Holiday Flavors and Favors

published by

THE JUNIOR LEAGUE OF GREENSBORO, INC.

Total Revision   July 1982   15,000

Proceeds from the sale of this book will be contributed to The Community Trust Fund of the Junior League of Greensboro, to finance projects in the community.

Printed in the United States of America

ISBN 0-9605788-1-1

Table of Contents

Special thanks go to those members and friends of the Junior League of Greensboro who tasted, tested and submitted recipes and ideas for our book. We regret that it was impossible to include all submissions and we ask your indulgence for the editorial liberties that were taken.

Holiday Flavors and Favors Committee

Foreword

Christmas joy is to be found in sharing one's time, talents, and thoughts with others. It is easy to lose sight of that simple maxim in the frenzy and furor that often accompanies the holiday season. Our hope is that **Holiday Flavors and Favors** will uncomplicate your Christmas entertaining and gift giving sufficiently to enable you to usher in the New Year with energy and enthusiasm.

Our "Gourmet Gatherings" section suggests a number of possible party plans for varying ages and occasions. Perhaps one or a combination of several will meet your particular needs. Each party plan includes a possible menu, invitation instructions, table decorations and serving suggestions. Those items listed on party menus are included by categories at the end of the section.

Recipes for food that may be given as gifts as well as instructions for packaging such food gifts are found in the "Greetings with Gifts" section of our book.

The intent of our book is to provide you with a guideline for holiday entertaining and gift giving. With just a little bit of pre-planning, your hostessing needn't be an awesome burden, nor need the selection and preparation of gifts for friends and family be a chore that leaves you destitute. We share these ideas with you with the hope that they will be useful and valuable. By your support you are contributing to the Community Trust Fund of the Junior League of Greensboro, N. C., Inc., and thereby sharing in the provision of goods and services that will be realized throughout our entire community in the areas of education, culture, health and welfare.

Copies of **Holiday Flavors and Favors** may be obtained by writing The Junior League of Greensboro, N. C., Inc., c/o **Holiday Flavors and Favors,** 113 N. Eugene St., Greensboro, North Carolina, 27401.

The purpose of the Association of Junior Leagues, Inc. is exclusively educational and charitable and is:

> to promote voluntarism,
>
> to develop the potential of its members for voluntary
>
> participation in community affairs,
>
> and
> to demonstrate the effectiveness of trained volunteers.

Gourmet Gatherings

PARTY AND CRAFT IDEAS

RECIPES

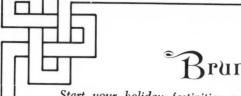

Brunch

Start your holiday festivities early in the season with a Christmas Brunch. Someone needs to get the ball rolling on holiday entertaining — why not you? Our suggestion is an easy party for you to prepare and a great way for you to say "Suddenly, it's Christmas."

INVITATIONS: Find a Christmas note card of the Grandma Moses or Currier and Ives variety depicting a snowy winter morning, preferably one without verse or message. Write your own message including all the necessary information as per the following examples: "Come in out of the cold for Brunch with the Morgans" or "Begin the holiday season with Brunch at the Morgans" or "Bundle up and venture out to Brunch at the Morgans" Saturday, December 6, 11:00 A.M.

MENU:

Rum Punch (p. 32)
Jenny's Eggs (p. 46)
Ham
Broiled Peaches (p. 49)
Moravian Sugar Cake
Orange Muffins (p. 52)

DECORATIONS: A lovely and long lasting decoration is the Apple Tree centerpiece. Though it takes a while to prepare, it is not difficult, and is as handsome a piece as ever decked a holiday table. This basic centerpiece can be varied by using yellow apples or lemons in a formal design, or a combination of other fruits including berries and grapes in a less structured design. You will need:

aluminum pie plate
sticky florist tape
1 tall block of soaked oasis
green floral chicken wire
16-18 red apples (slightly different sizes)

green wooden floral picks
1 fresh pineapple
American boxwood sprigs and 1 dozen magnolia leaves submerged in water 3 hrs. to condition

With aluminum pie plate as a base, use sticky florist tape to attach oasis, covered with chicken wire, by winding tape through the wire, pulling tight, and sticking the tape across the bottom of the pan. Do this on all sides. Apply Wesson Oil to apples to make them shine. Build up three tiers of apples, resting the first tier on the edge of the pie plate. Poke picks diagonally through base of apples and stick end of pick into oasis at a sharp angle. This leaves stem ends of apples sticking straight out. Poke sprigs of boxwood straight into oasis, being careful to fill in below the first tier of apples as well as in between. Use shorter sprigs at top. Cut off the bottom ⅔ of a fresh pineapple. (Cut can be sealed with paraffin, foil, or Saran, but not necessary.) Poke two picks into base of top part, about 2″ apart. Push the picks into top of oasis until pineapple top is secure on the top. Fill in around base of pineapple with boxwood. On the table, place magnolia leaves in a circle pointing out from the apple cone in a flower petal design.

Mrs. Samuel D. Hummel

SERVING SUGGESTIONS: If you have special Christmas china, it would be particularly welcome here. Wrap silverware in linen napkins and tie with red or green velvet ribbon. Serve buffet style.

Mrs. Thomas R. Beard

Wine Collection Party

This party provides an inexpensive yet elegant way to have a good time. Because invitees generally supply superb wines, good conversation among the guests and much mingling about while tasting and testing wine samples can be assured.

INVITATIONS: For a unique party invitation try to create a mock billing letter on which is conveyed the essential party details. For example: "Farrell's Collection Agency" will mark your account past due as of 8:00 P.M. Saturday, Dec. 20th if a bottle of your favorite wine and your company is not present at 4503 Cornell Drive.

MENU:
Selected Wines
Caviar Cheese Spread and Rye Wafers (p. 38)
Shrimp in Butter & Lemon
Melon Wrapped in Ham or Prosciutto
Chicken Liver Paté
Crusty Bread & Butter
Cheeses (Brie, Boursin, Muenster, Gouda, Cheese Fondue) and Crackers
Sliced Fruits: Apples, Pears, Bananas, Grapes

DECORATIONS: For a lovely centerpiece these twin Topiary Trees couldn't be simpler or more effective. They will last up to 10 days providing continuing pleasure even after the party is over.

Materials Needed:

2 low bowls	greening pins
2 24″ dowels	red grosgrain ribbon
sphagnum moss	gingham ribbon made into small bows
2 needle point holders	fresh or artificial cranberries
floral clay	fresh camellia leaves, boxwood & ivy
floral picks	

DIRECTIONS: Form a ball of sphagnum moss; wrap and tie with string; soak thoroughly in water. Using greening pins, attach greenery to the ball of moss. Using the picks, attach the bows and cranberries to the ball. Impale the ball securely on red grosgrain wrapped dowel. Use the floral clay to secure the needlepoint holders in the low bowl. Insert ends of dowel into the needlepoints, disguised with short stems of ivy or other left over greenery. Repeat for twin.

Mrs. Donald F. Orr

SERVING SUGGESTIONS: Host should have a minimum of two bottles appetizer wine, 2 bottles white wine, 2 bottles rosé, 2 bottles red and 2 bottles dessert wine. Though they may not be needed, these wines should be on hand to accompany the various foods on your menu. Be certain, if you should deviate from the suggested menu, not to serve foods which outshine the wines. Foods such as vinegar, heavy spices, asparagus, citrus fruits, strong or salty dips, and strong fish should be avoided. Foods and the wines that compliment them can be arranged attractively around topiary trees centerpiece on one large table. It may suit your circumstances better to use center piece on single table and set up various auxiliary tables with food and wines artfully arranged. Either approach is satisfactory.

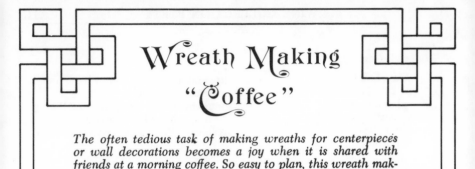

Wreath Making
"Coffee"

The often tedious task of making wreaths for centerpieces or wall decorations becomes a joy when it is shared with friends at a morning coffee. So easy to plan, this wreath making party is a "must" for your holiday entertaining.

INVITATIONS: Cut wreath shape out of green construction paper. Cut ¼" red satin ribbon into small strip and tie into a bow. Staple bow to top of wreath. Cut a white construction paper circle to fill center of wreath, and paste to the back. Write party information and instructions on white center. Fold in half and place in envelope. Instruct each person to bring her own wreath form and sufficient ribbon, bows, and/or anything else she may need in order to create her own distinctive wreath.

MENU:	**Coffee Punch (p. 34)**
	Date Bars (p. 80)
	Nancy Foxworth's Pumpkin Bread (p. 70)
	Pecan Squares (p. 55)
	Sour Cream Coffeecake (p. 58)

DECORATIONS AND SERVING SUGGESTIONS: For serving table centerpiece buy medium sized artificial wreath from florist. Make about 24 bows from colorful calico, gingham and plaid Christmas ribbon and attach to wreath by using florist wire in this way: Wrap wire first around center of bow, then around a sprig of greenery on wreath. Space bows evenly around wreath. Place wreath flat on table and set large wide candle in center. Make the refreshment area convenient to your work area. Since the party is informal, you may want to use plastic holiday glasses and paper dessert plates. Have on hand the materials necessary for guests to use in wreath making. Set table or tables up in an area that can take the punishment of creative craft-making. You will need to supply adequate lighting, scissors, floral wire and picks, pinking shears, wire cutters, greenery, some extra bow making ribbon or fabric and a lot of moral support. If you have the time and are especially creative yourself, you may wish to have some sample wreaths on hand to trigger the imagination of your guests.

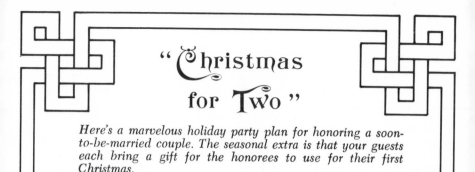

"Christmas for Two"

Here's a marvelous holiday party plan for honoring a soon-to-be-married couple. The seasonal extra is that your guests each bring a gift for the honorees to use for their first Christmas.

INVITATIONS: Using Christmas postcards "Xerox" the illustrated design onto the cards. Write in the following message: Join us for dinner, honoring Jane Blake and Robert Johnson. Friday, December 20, 7:30 P.M. Please bring a gift for Jane and Robert to use for their first Christmas.

MENU: Cocktails
Chicken Livers Hors D'oeuvres (p. 35) Cheese Puffs (p. 83)
Wild Rice and Shrimp Casserole (p. 44)
Tomatoes Stuffed with Spinach Soufflé (p. 49)
Watercress and Orange Salad (p. 48)
French Bread Pouilly-Fuisse Wine
Limelight Pie (p. 60) or Strawberry-Banana Pie (p. 61)
Coffee and Cordials

DECORATIONS: What more appropriate decoration to greet guests at your front door at such a party than a Christmas Kissing Ball. This lovely entrance hall decoration can be quickly and simply made using the following instructions. Materials needed: 1 apple, enough boxwood sprigs to cover apple, mistletoe, hair pins, velvet ribbon or yarn. Stick boxwood sprigs into apple securing with hair pins if necessary. When completely covered trim uneven leaves with scissors so that a circle is formed. Cut ribbon into three long strips. Tie around ball leaving enough at the top to form a loop to attach to a chandelier. Tie loops together next to top of ball. Make a small bow at the bottom of the ball with the six ends of the ribbon. Attach mistletoe sprig to the bow. Moisture in the apple will keep greens fresh for at least a week.

An example of a handmade decoration to be given to the honorees for their Christmas tree is a sand dollar ornament. Take a sand dollar and bleach it in Clorox; then let dry in the sun. Run a red or green ribbon through a hole in the top and hang it on the tree.

SERVING SUGGESTIONS: The menu cited is well suited for either a buffet or sit down dinner. Gift opening should be reserved for after the meal, perhaps while enjoying after dinner drinks.

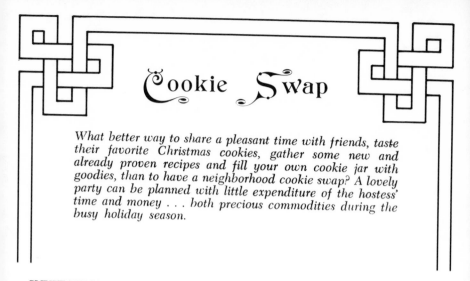

Cookie Swap

What better way to share a pleasant time with friends, taste their favorite Christmas cookies, gather some new and already proven recipes and fill your own cookie jar with goodies, than to have a neighborhood cookie swap? A lovely party can be planned with little expenditure of the hostess' time and money . . . both precious commodities during the busy holiday season.

INVITATIONS: Use a 3 x 5 recipe card and write: Bring 3 dozen of your favorite Christmas cookies and the recipe; join us for a "Cookie Swap" on Dec. 2, 1975 at 10:30 A.M., Circle Drive.

MENU:

Eggnog (p. 32)
Cookies — brought by your guests
Jello Strawberries (p. 55)

DECORATIONS AND SERVING SUGGESTIONS: Set up long table with cloth and centerpiece of a barren branch of a tree on which cookie cutters are tied with colorful ribbons. Matching runner of ribbon or fabric can be placed the long way on the cloth. Have on hand extra containers to receive guests' cookies, in case what they have brought them in is not suitable. Provide recipe cards and pens so your guests can copy the recipes that interest them. Collect children's shoe boxes prior to the party and cover with brown mailing paper. As each guest leaves, tie a Christmas calico ribbon around his "Cookie Swap" collection.

Della Robbia Cocktail Party

The special touch for this Christmas cocktail party is the addition of the "Della Robbia" theme which is subtly carried throughout the menu, invitations and decoration. The party offers a change of pace from the routine cocktail party and requires no bartending.

INVITATIONS: Purchase or make a round card with Della Robbia wreath as the outer rim. Invitations can then be printed or handwritten inside.

MENU:

Fish House Punch (p. 34)	Cocktail Franks (p. 37)
Ham Biscuits	Sardine Ball and Crackers (p. 39)
Hot Broccoli Dip & Fritos (p. 38)	Gin Spread and Crackers (p. 39)
Marinated Artichokes (p. 49)	Vegetables with Curry Dip (p. 40)

Walnut-Brandy Balls (p. 80)

DECORATIONS: Decorations through the house will be fruit and greenery — using real lemons, limes, apples, crabapples, oranges, grapes, small magnolia leaves and evergreens. Make Della Robbia wreaths for doors, around candles, over mantels etc. Apple or lemon tree (page 9) would be appropriate also. Fruit is beautiful on a mantel and/or wound around banister on a greenery rope. The really smashing feature of your buffet table is the ice mold in the Fish House Punch. It can be made simply the day before the party by doing the following: In a 2½ gallon paper ice cream container make a layer of mixed fruit in the bottom. Pack ice cubes on top to hold fruit down. Arrange another layer of fruit and add more ice. Continue until carton is nearly full. Fill to top with cold water and freeze. Take from freezer 1 hour before party time to thaw slightly. Peel cardboard from mold and place ice block in super wide punch bowl. Drape grapes over the top of mold. Fill bowl with Fish House Punch. Decorate with extra fruit around base of bowl.

Mrs. John T. Gregory

Family
Decorations Dinner

A fun party for children and grown ups alike is one in which both can participate in a creative activity. Share a Christmas time meal with neighbors, friends and their families and at the same time make lovely and lasting decorations to be enjoyed throughout the holidays. Children will concentrate on making decorations for out-of-doors animal Christmas tree. Adults work on special family picture ornament or candy calendar.

INVITATION: Cut Christmas tree shape from green construction paper. From white paper cut the same shape but smaller. Glue the white shape on top of the green and write invitation. You will have to make invitation large enough to accommodate message; then fold and place in green or white envelope. Message:

Holiday fun is surely in store,
for all who enter our front door!
Make decorations for your Christmas tree,
And stay for supper with our family.

Sunday	December 20	5:00 P.M.	The Millers

MENU: **Gin Surprise (p. 31)**   **Cranberry Punch (p. 34)**
Assorted "Easy" Hors D'oeuvres (p. 35)
Potato Soup or Clam Bisque (p. 45)
Asparagus Salad (p. 48)
Mushroom Sandwiches (p. 36)   **Angels on Horseback (p. 46)**
Rosie's Chocolate Cake (p. 58)

DECORATIONS: Animal Tree — Children's out-of-doors animal tree can be decorated with strings of popcorn and cranberries, apple quarters, nuts, etc. Have on hand carpet thread and large eyed needles. Make large knot at end of thread and alternate popcorn and cranberries or make long string of either. Individual strings can be connected and swirled around tree. For added interest spear apple quarters with large eyed needles threaded with red or green yarn. Tie on tree.

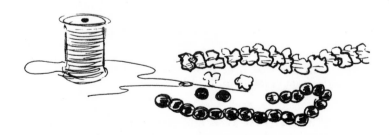

Family Portrait Ornament — You will need to have on hand Polaroid camera and film, wooden curtain rod rings, white acrylic paint, cardboard, glue, felt and ¼" wide red or green velvet ribbon. Keep men busy taking pictures of other families while wives make the rest of the ornament. Paint rings white. Cut cardboard in circle to fit size of ring. Cut photograph and glue to cardboard circle. Glue photo onto back of ring so it is framed by the ring. Tie ribbon (glue at intervals) around the outside of ring. Make small bow at top. Attach "Santa Helper" at center of bow.

By Barbara Rettenbach

Candy Calendar — You can speed up the operation of making candy calendars by precutting and packaging the materials. It might simplify matters if you sew braid on strips before guests arrive or designate one of your guests as head "seamstress" once the craft making commences.

For each calendar you will need:

    felt strip, (36" by 5") of red, white or green felt
    cardboard tube from coat hanger
    plastic name tag holders with pin on back (may be obtained from
        office supply company)
    24 pieces wrapped peppermint candy
    yarn (different color from felt strip)
    braid (contrasting color from felt strip)
    one small bell   large crewel type needle

Cut felt into strips, making a point at the bottom. Sew braid or rick rack down both sides of felt and around point. Sew bell approximately 1" from bottom of point. Type or print the following poem on name tag holder and place in plastic holder:

December first to Christmas	So this little strip of felt
is the longest time of year.	will tell you the exact amount.
It seems as 'tho Santa,	Untie a bow every night
never will appear.	when the Sandman casts his spell,
How many days 'til Christmas?	and Christmas will be here
It's mighty hard to count.	by the time you reach the bell.

Merry Christmas

Measure down the middle of strip of felt and make 24 marks with chalk or pencil (approximately 1" to 1½" apart.).
Using a large needle, insert yarn (cut into 10" strips) into chalk marks. 24 strips of yarn should be down the front of each felt strip so that candy may be tied into it. Roll the top of felt strips over a cardboard tube (cut same width as the felt) and glue felt to tube. Let glue dry thoroughly. Cut a longer strip of yarn (approx. 16") and run through cardboard tube for hanging. Tie a bow into top of yarn. Place poem on front of felt directly under where felt is rolled over tube. Tie 24 pieces of candy into yarn pieces down the front of felt strip. Tie a bow with the yarn.

Olive B. Jordan

SERVING SUGGESTIONS: Keep this party very casual using mugs for soup and pottery type plates if you have them. Fill a big soup tureen and cover and keep sandwiches on a hot tray. Encourage guests to serve themselves when they come to a break in the making of the decorations.

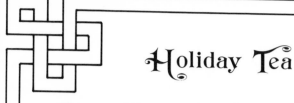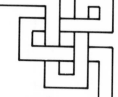

Holiday Tea

Honor a neighbor, special friend or house guest, or simply usher in the season with an afternoon tea. The great thing about this menu is that all items can be prepared ahead of time leaving you free to do some shopping, decorating, or simply relax the morning of your party.

INVITATIONS: Secure postcard edged in red or green (ones that come with their own envelopes). Staple a tea bag, or stylistic facsimile to one side of the front. To the side write the following message: Come for Tea!   301 Chestnut St.   Dec. 15   4:00   Lib Brewer

MENU: Plain and Russian Tea (p. 66)
                        Shrimp Spread with Crackers
        Cranberry Nut Bread Spread with Cream Cheese (p. 59)
                        Lemon Bars (p. 79)
              Spiced Nuts (p. 81)   Buckeyes (p. 54)

DECORATIONS: Paint a medium sized basket white. Let dry. Using oil paints (whatever colors you desire) and a small brush (watercolor size), paint an abstract design (flowers, flame stitch, etc.) on the outside of the basket. Allow to dry and spray with clear shellac. Fill basket with pine cones. Tie large bow, of one of the colors used in the painting, to the handle.
Using a gingham, solid or print fabric that complements the painted basket centerpiece, cut 12″ square pieces with pinking shears. Fold and use as napkins.

Mrs. William T. Martin

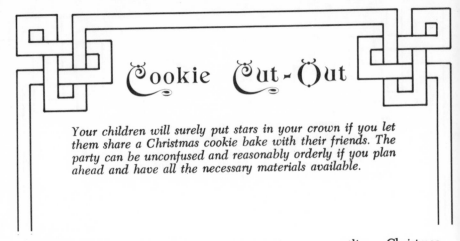

Cookie Cut-Out

Your children will surely put stars in your crown if you let them share a Christmas cookie bake with their friends. The party can be unconfused and reasonably orderly if you plan ahead and have all the necessary materials available.

INVITATIONS: Using red or green construction paper outline a Christmas cookie cutter on paper and cut. Write message on the shape and put in envelopes: Come to a Cookie Cutout! (time, place, and signature).

MENU:
Peppermint Punch (p. 34)
Degas Dish (p. 43)   Tossed Green Salad
Hot Rolls (p. 52)
Snowballs (p. 56)   or   Yuletide Chocolate Dessert (p. 53)

DECORATIONS: Virtually no decorations are needed as there will be "decoration" enough once the kids go creative! You may want to set up this table with Christmas theme matching paper cloth, napkins, plates, and cups. A cute centerpiece would be this Toy Block Tree. The bright colors make skill almost unnecessary for a charming effect and anyone can stack blocks. You will need: 1) playschool wooden blocks in decorative colors, 2) small wooden angel or Santa Claus for top of tree, 3) packages of cloth leaves with stems cut off, 4) assorted ½″ wooden figures to decorate tree, 5) packages of small papier maché fruit, 6) package of ½″ Christmas balls, 7) shirt cardboard, 8) small acorns and pine cones, gilded, 9) Elmer's glue.

For a large tree arrange 10 blocks in a circle spelling out your last name or initials on front side with blocks. Cut piece of cardboard the size of the circle. Glue bottom of blocks to cardboard. Next glue a ring of 7 blocks to top of 10 blocks, to form second layer. Let dry thoroughly. Repeat with layer of five blocks, then three, then one. Vary colors as you go. Glue cloth leaves in the angled junctures of blocks. Push in and hold a few minutes until set. Decorate trees with small animals, toy figures, fruit and Christmas balls. Glue angel or Santa Claus on top. Dry overnight. Trees may be any size; simply alter number of layers.

PROCEDURE: Set up 2 or 3 uncrowded work areas at which children can roll out dough and decorate cookies. Use cookie mix recipe (p. 56) or purchase refrigerator sugar cookie dough. Once the dough is rolled out, children can cut cookies to whatever shape they like and decorate to suit their fancy. Have on hand lots of colored sugar decorations. Children will love monitoring the baking of their masterpieces too. A nice touch would be for children to deliver their creations to special neighbors, children in day care centers, sick friends, shut-ins, senior citizens or anyone else who might enjoy a gift box of cookies. You may add another dimension to the party by having a few of the guests to decorate gift boxes. After the meal, the guests can put cookies in boxes, tie them with pretty ribbon and deliver.

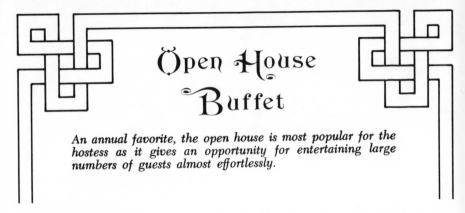

Open House Buffet

An annual favorite, the open house is most popular for the hostess as it gives an opportunity for entertaining large numbers of guests almost effortlessly.

INVITATIONS: In advance of the season have picture of host and hostess made while standing at opened, decorated-for-Christmas front door. Print photo on Christmas card and write invitation beside picture as follows.

Open House Buffet
7:00 until
December 23rd
The Borden's

MENU: **Serve Yourself Bar**
Chili-Cheese Log and Crackers (p. 40)   Marinated Shrimp (p. 40)
Chicken Casserole (p. 43)
Ham-Veal Meat Loaf (p. 41)
Blue-Cheese and Bacon Potatoes (p. 50)
Pea Salad (p. 48)
Chocolate Cheesecake (p. 60)
Sugar Plum Cake (p. 59)

SERVING SUGGESTIONS: Set up serve yourself bar wherever appropriate in your home. Be certain to provide protective covering for wood tables. Have usual mixers and water, but, in addition, mix up pitchers of mixers for whiskey sours, martinis, and some other favorites. You may wish to include an original or unique concoction for the more adventuresome. Have hot trays ready to receive chicken casserole and ham-veal loaf. Other items should hold up well.

DECORATIONS: Tie gingham, calico or plaid ribbon in bows on chandelier. Attach a larger bow at each corner of serving table. Use a full, beautiful fern in a silver container for a centerpiece. Group various sizes and colors of candles on mantels in living room and den. Place sprigs of greenery around and between candles. An especially effective touch would be to use real candles in your windows. This can be done safely when candles are set in tin tart pans with drapes well away from the flame. Line both sides of front walk with candles. Set candles in 6″ clay pots filled with sand to hold candle firmly. Place hurricane lantern over top and tie ribbon around rim of clay pot.

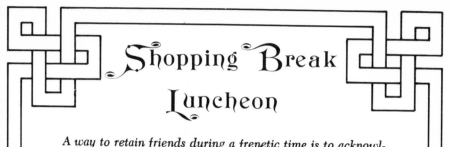

Shopping Break Luncheon

A way to retain friends during a frenetic time is to acknowledge their busy schedules in planning your party. This luncheon is as fun a party to arrange as to attend and your guests will be delighted by your efforts to accommodate them during the "hectic holidays." Most of the menu can be completely prepared the day before. Quiche ingredients are prepared ahead and combined at the last minute.

INVITATIONS: Write your invitations on a small brown lunch bag. Attach rope handles to simulate shopping bags. Fold and place in standard sized envelope. Invite your guest for "around noon", which gives them some flexibility if they're held up in long lines or traffic. Drinks can be served over a period of ½ hour and that amount of time should be sufficient for everyone to arrive.

MENU:
Wassail Punch (p. 32)
Hot Clam Dip and Crackers or Chips (p. 36)
Quiche (p. 46)   or   Assorted Sandwich Makings
Congealed Broccoli Salad (p. 47)
Fudge Cupcakes (p. 57)   or   Pecan Tarts (p. 54)

DECORATIONS: Place small Christmas tree in center of serving table. Decorate tree with small shopping lists, Alka-Seltzer tablets, corn plasters, calendars with days marked off, tiny wrapped packages etc. On the wall hang shopping bags from local stores.

SERVING SUGGESTIONS: Place quiche on hot tray and arrange other dishes attractively on serving table. To add to informality encourage guests to prepare their plates when it suits them. You may want to use plastic plates and cups in holiday patterns or colors. Keep it simple so guests won't feel uncomfortable breezing in and "eating and running".

Mrs. John W. Black

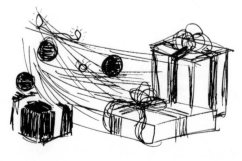

Caroling Party

*What better way to share your Christmas spirit than by rais-
ing your voices in song with neighbors and friends. An
especially nice tradition is the making of a ribbon wreath,
created by forming a wire coat hanger into a wreath shape.
At each home visited carolers beg for ribbon. They then tie
ribbon in bows on wreath. By the end of the caroling the
wreath should be full of color. Ask guests to suggest names
of a shut-in, nursing home or hospital to which the wreath
will be taken to decorate the door.*

INVITATIONS: Using a Christmas caroling book of the sort given away
by companies at Christmas time, staple a sheet of paper to the front page
stating: "Bring this book with you to Paige and John Griffins', 7:00,
December 22nd, 1612 Sunset Drive, and we'll go caroling. Plenty of
warming food and drink promised. Regrets only: 252-1222

MENU: Swedish Glogg (p. 33)
          Shrimp Ball (p. 39)   Cheese Cubes (p. 37)
     Boeuf Bourguignon (p. 41)   or   Chicken Spaghetti (p. 43)
               Corn and Bean Casserole (p. 50)
                      Beer Muffins (p. 52)
     Noel Bars (p. 54)   Cranberry Upside Down Cake (p. 58)
                      Plenty of Hot Coffee

DECORATIONS: Place a Bakers Clay Wreath on the center of your table
which has been covered with a red table cloth. Use four red candles in the
wreath.

Bakers Clay or Golden Wreath

Materials Needed:

Bread Dough — 4 cups flour, 1 cup salt, 1½ cups warm water, 1 tsp. instant tea (heaping)

Mix flour and salt. Mix instant tea and water. Let cool. Combine two mixtures and mix well with hands. Knead until smooth and cover with plastic wrap.

aluminum foil, knives, toothpicks, cookie sheet

whole cloves
varnish or shellac

Cover cookie sheet with aluminum foil and preheat oven to 300°. Pinch a large piece of dough and roll into a sausage shape. Wet ends and press together forming a circle (8" diameter, 5" inner diameter, ½" thick). Place on cookie sheet. Roll out enough dough for several leaves ¼" thick. Cut into leaf shapes and score with knife for veins. Moisten back of each leaf and press onto wreath. Make large fruit next (apples, pears, peaches). Press whole cloves into dough for stems and core end of fruit. Wet wreath circle and attach fruits. Make small fruits (apples, pears, peaches) and imprint textures with toothpick or fork. Attach to wreath filling in spaces*. Make a bow from ¼" thick strip of dough. Place on separate foil covered sheet. Bake wreath and bow for 3 hours at 300°. Place on wire rack and let cool for 2-3 days. Coat wreath and bow with shellac or varnish. When dry attach bow with epoxy cement.

*Can be made with indentions for candles to use as centerpiece to be made at this point.

Mrs. A. Ritchie Lewis

SERVING SUGGESTIONS: Serve Glogg, shrimp garnished with holly, and cheese cubes as your guests arrive. At 8:00 P.M. begin the caroling, making sure you have flashlights for carolers and an established route to follow. When carolers return serve remainder of menu buffet style. Provide separate plates for dessert.

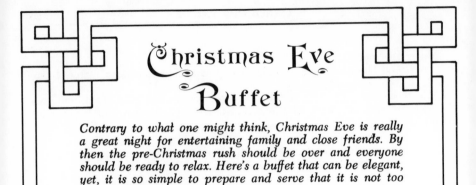

Christmas Eve Buffet

Contrary to what one might think, Christmas Eve is really a great night for entertaining family and close friends. By then the pre-Christmas rush should be over and everyone should be ready to relax. Here's a buffet that can be elegant, yet, it is so simple to prepare and serve that it is not too taxing for the hostess.

INVITATIONS: Handwritten invitations on seasonal paper or cards might include something like:

On the night before Christmas
At our house please pause —
With food, drink and fellowship
We'll wait for Santa Claus.
7:30   The Murphys

MENU:
Champagne Punch (p. 32)
Spinach Spread & Crackers (p. 39)   Deviled Ham Puffs (p. 36)
Mother's Scalloped Oysters (p. 44)
Tomato-Pear Pork Chop Casserole (p. 44)
Potato Soufflé (p. 51)
Raspberry Congealed Salad (p. 47)
Black Forest Torte (p. 57)   Texas Pudding (p. 53)

DECORATIONS: Fill a champagne cooler or silver bowl with red carnations for a lovely centerpiece. They seem to last forever. Set up card tables around the house, cover with red, white, or green cloths and mark places for guests with Angel Place Markers. Directions for these markers, which would make delightful favors for your guests, follow. Your guests' name may be painted onto skirt of angel or written on paper and glued to skirt.

Using clean tin can lids (from juice or large food cans) cut with tin snips on solid lines shown in diagram. Shape into angel, bending back large section for skirt, bending arms forward to hold two small candles, and bending back wings and head.

Christmas Dinner

Perhaps this, the most special family gathering of the year, will take on a new and even more significant glow if you widen your family circle to include others whose Christmas might otherwise be a lonesome occasion. Share your Christmas spirit with a shut in, senior citizen or college student unable to get home for the holidays, and your own joy will be multiplied.

INVITATIONS: Invitations can be made by telephone to family members as well as other invitees.

MENU: Crabmeat Dip and Crackers or Potato Chips (p. 37)
Apricot Congealed Salad (p. 47)
Leg of Lamb (p. 41)
Brown Rice (p. 51)   Burgundy Beets (p. 50)
Spinach-Artichoke Casserole (p. 50)   Hot Rolls (p. 52)
Choice of: Rum Pudding (p. 53), French Silk Pie (p. 62), Pumpkin Pie (p. 61)
Kahluha (p. 31)

DECORATIONS: As a centerpiece on your Christmas table may we suggest placing a medium sized poinsettia plant in a decorative cachè pot.

The directions for such a container are as follows:
1 cylindrical pot with straight sides
Ribbon: (should be of various textures such as picot, grosgrain, satin — should use only one pattern such as plaid, stripe, or polka dot per pot to avoid too busy a look)
a. 2 types ribbon 1″ wide
b. 1 type of any width between 1″ and 3″ depending on the height of the pot
c. 1 type ¼″ wide
Elmer's glue   Scotchgard spray
felt circle size of pot bottom

Cut ribbon "type a" in strips measuring height of pot plus 1". Cut enough to alternate the two types of ribbon "a" around pot with edges touching. Apply thin line of glue around top of pot, let dry slightly and attach tops of ribbon strips. Do not overlap. Continue until entire pot is covered with strips hanging lengthwise. Make sure ribbons are straight up and down. If ribbons don't fit exactly you may have to use a different sized one at the end. Cut at least two lengths of ribbon "type b" equal to distance around pot. Attach one end of the ribbon to side of pot near the top. Weave in and out of lengthwise strips and attach other end under ribbon. Repeat with second strip. You may use as many strips as size of pot and ribbon permits. Pull ends of ribbon "a" under pot firmly and glue. Glue felt circle to bottom. Glue ¼" ribbon around top of pot and tie in bow. Spray with Scotchgard. Be careful not to get glue on ribbon.

Mrs. James M. Dowtin, Jr.

At each table setting place a tiny basket filled with nuts or mints. Tie a small bow of one of the same ribbons used in the cache pot on each basket and attach a Christmas gift tag bearing the name of whom is to be seated there.

SERVING SUGGESTIONS: We recommend that Christmas dinner be a sitdown affair with plates served at the table. You may wish to serve the desserts buffet style and the cordial would be elegant served in the living room after the meal. Changing the serving center will do wonders for fidgety kids and allows you to enjoy your home in its Christmas decor even more fully.

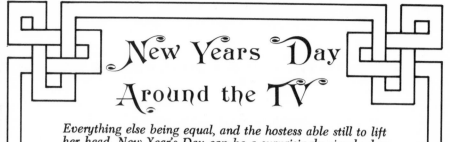

New Years Day Around the TV

Everything else being equal, and the hostess able still to lift her head, New Year's Day can be a surprisingly simple day on which to entertain. The entertainment for the occasion is well supplied by T.V. football, so all that is left for you is the preparation of the meal and a few simple decorations.

INVITATIONS: Staple packaged Alka Seltzer tablet to the front of a plain informal. On the inside, write:

TAKE THIS IMMEDIATELY UPON RISING
ON JANUARY 1st
1976
THEN JOIN US FOR THE BALLGAMES 11:00

Susan & Jim Thomas
2317 Kirkpatrick Place

MENU:

Borden's Bloody Marys (p. 33)
Miniature Quiche (p. 35)
New Year's Chicken (p. 42)   Strawberry Congealed Salad (p. 47)
Homemade Hot Rolls (p. 52)
Cheesecake (p. 59)   or   Holland Ice Box Cake (p. 57)
Lots of Hot Coffee

DECORATIONS: T.V. Tray Placemats: Using felt in the school colors of your guest make a placemat 12" x 16". Cut a small 3" x 5" football shaped pocket of felt. Glue to the lower right hand corner of the mat to hold silverware.
Centerpiece for Table and/or T.V.: Make an arrangement of fresh boxwood. Make college flags using felt and tall floral picks. Insert into arrangement.

SERVING SUGGESTIONS: Serve Bloody Marys and Miniature Quiche as soon as guests begin to arrive. Retain food until about 1:30 or 2:00 so guests will not have to be fed again before the ball games are over.

The parties listed below are meant as a springboard for your imagination. Choose recipes from the pages to come, add a few frills, and take all the credit for a unique entertaining idea.

GRANDMOTHERS TREAT

If you have recently become a grandmother, this party should receive star billing on your holiday calendar. Plan to invite grandmothers, mothers, and children of your close friends for a **brief** afternoon get-together, about the time families arrive in town for Christmas. One, to one and a half hours is about all the time the nerves and the house can stand for such an event, but seeing and showing off all the new additions is well worth the strain. So you can enjoy the event, be sure to put all valuables well out of reach. Serve the children cans of baby juice, from a silver tray, and Christmas cookies, and they should be quite content. Mothers and grandmothers may need something a little stronger. Provide light finger foods to suit the time of day. This party is a real treat for friends who have moved out of town and don't get to see each other often.

AROUND THE WORLD PROGRESSIVE DINNER

This party is especially nice because it relieves the hostesses of the burden of preparing an entire meal, allows for the gathering of a large group of people, and enables guests to see many of their friends' lovely Christmas decorations. Get together with friends over coffee and decide on the number of courses to be served. Recruit a hostess for each course. Next, decide on various countries to be represented by each course. Each hostess should serve a dish representative of that country and have some decorations in her home that are traditional for her country. A centerpiece typifying the country would be nice. For invitations draw a world map numbering the stops along the way.

BLACK TIE DINNER

Many individuals enjoy dressing formally on occasion. If you find yourself and several friends in this group, you may wish to celebrate the holidays with a formal affair. Use all of your very best linens, silver, china, and crystal. Splurge, if you do not normally have help, and hire some for this evening. You may wish to fix all the food in advance and have your help put on the finishing touches and serve. Candlelight, a fire in the fireplace, fine wines and perhaps some champagne will assure an evening your guests will long remember.

GIN SURPRISE

This drink would be especially tasty if you have received a basket of grape-fruit and want to squeeze them to substitute for the canned juice. (Good project for the children!) Expect guests to drink 1 pint of liquid or more and vary recipe to fit your needs.

2 cans (1 qt. 14 oz.) unsweetened grapefruit juice
1 fifth gin   red and green cheeries

Combine juice and gin. Garnish with cherries frozen in ice cubes.

MRS. JAMES E. BETTS

KAHLUHA

What could be more special than a homemade cordial. Great for serving or giving to close friends.

6 T. instant coffee
1½ qt. water
4 T. vanilla
1 qt. 190 proof alcohol

6 oz. pure glycerin
1 qt. water
6 cups sugar

Dissolve coffee in 1½ qt. water. Add vanilla, alcohol and glycerin. Make simple syrup by combining 1 qt. water and 6 cups sugar. Boil 5 minutes. Let cool. Combine all and bottle. Let sit for at least two weeks.

MRS. GEORGE KLICK, HENDERSONVILLE, N.C.

CHAMPAGNE PUNCH

This punch is beautiful in a large silver bowl with a fancy ice block floating in it. One-half of the preparation can be done the day before. This recipe serves ten, quadruple for fifty.

1½ cups powdered sugar
½ cup Triple Sec or orange liqueur
½ cup Cognac
½ cup maraschino cherry juice
    cherries (optional)

3 bottles champagne
1 orange sliced
1 lemon sliced
1 qt. pineapple sherbet

Combine the sugar, liqueur, Cognac, cherry juice, and cherries, if desired. Just before serving add remaining ingredients.

MRS. RICHARD HALL

RUM PUNCH

Watch out!

1 qt. apple juice
1 qt. cranberry juice
¼ cup real lemon juice

1 fifth light rum
green cherries
sliced orange with peel

Combine ingredients in punch bowl. Cherries and/or orange slices may be frozen in ice or floated on top. The green cherries add Christmas color to the red punch.

OLIVE JORDAN

HOT WASSAIL

1 gallon apple cider
1 cup cranberry juice
1 large #5 can of apricot nectar
1 large #5 can of pineapple juice
1 T. whole cloves

1 box stick cinnamon
1 cup sugar
½ cup lemon juice
rum or brandy

Combine first 8 ingredients. Simmer one hour. Add rum or brandy (may substitute flavoring) to taste. Float small baked apples on top of wassail in punch bowl. Serve warm.

MRS. WILLIAM WILKERSON

EGG NOG

How can one get through the holidays without egg nog? This recipe is well worth the twenty minutes it takes to prepare it.

1 dozen egg yolks
1 scant cup sugar
1 fifth whiskey or bourbon
    (for ½ recipe use 12 oz.)

½ cup rum
1 quart milk
1 quart ½&½ cream
1 pint cream (whipped)

Beat egg yolks adding sugar to taste. Stir in whiskey slowly, then rum. Add milk and ½ & ½ cream. At last add whipped cream. Sprinkle top with nutmeg if desired.

MRS. EDWIN S. MELVIN

GLOGG

This warm drink is perfect for a cold night. Make it the day before and warm before serving.

3 whole cardamons
8 whole cloves
1 cinnamon stick
4 inch strip of orange rind
1⅓ cup water
¼ cup blanched almonds

½ cup golden raisins
1 bottle (24 oz.) Bordeaux wine
1 bottle (24 oz.) Port wine
½ pt. brandy
sugar to taste

Tie cardamons, cloves, cinnamon, and orange rind in cheesecloth bag. Place water and bag in pan. Bring to a boil. Simmer covered for 10 min. Add almonds and raisins and simmer 10 minutes longer. Add Bordeaux, Port, and brandy and bring to a quick boil. Remove from heat immediately. Cool and store covered overnight at serving time; remove spice bag. Heat Glogg, but do not boil. Add sugar to taste. Serve in heated mugs or glasses with a few almonds and raisins in each glass.

MRS. WILLIAM VAN LEUVEN, PRINCETON, N.J.

BORDEN'S BLOODY MARY

This recipe is for one drink so increase the quantity to suit your needs. Once tasted, you'll "need" a lot. You may substitute Gin for Vodka.

2 oz. V-8 juice
2 oz. tomato juice (or
  Beefamato juice)
⅛ fresh lemon (juice)
2 dashes Worcestershire Sauce

4 drops Tobasco (or to taste)
1 pinch garlic salt
1 pinch ground fresh black
  pepper
1 oz. of Vodka or more to taste

Combine all ingredients but Vodka. Just before serving add Vodka. If desired, garnish with celery stalk, slice of cucumber or thin slice of lemon.

ROBERT H. BORDEN

FISH HOUSE PUNCH

Using this festive punch allows for a nice change of pace from the ordinary cocktails. No bartender is needed and this recipe will serve up to 30 average drinkers.

fresh apples, lemons, oranges, limes and grapes°
1 quart lemon juice (frozen and sweetened)
2 quarts Jamaican rum   ¾ cup peach brandy
1 quart Cognac   2 quarts water

Thaw lemon juice. Add rum, cognac, brandy and water. Mix well. May need to stir occassionally if used during party.
° See "Della Robia Cocktail Party" for directions on how to use fruit to make ice mold for punch.

MRS. JOHN T. GREGORY

COFFEE PUNCH

Such a delightful change for a "Coffee!" Even non-coffee drinkers love it. Serves 20 people, 1½ cups.

20 cups of coffee
½ gallon ice cream (slightly softened), vanilla
1 cup whipping cream (whipped) or more to taste

Cool coffee to lukewarm. Mash up ice cream in punch bowl. Pour coffee over ice cream and stir. Top with whipped cream.

MRS. G. K. LEEMON, JR., ASHEVILLE, N.C.

CRANBERRY PUNCH

Colorful punch for children during the holidays. You may want to add vodka to spice it up for adults.

1 large bottle cranapple juice   1 cup fresh orange juice
orange slices

Combine juices. Garnish with orange slice placed in each glass of ice. Pour over ice.

PEPPERMINT PUNCH

A real treat for the little ones during the holidays.

1½ pints soft vanilla ice cream   1½ cups heavy cream, whipped
6 cups eggnog   ½ cup broken peppermint sticks
5¼ cups chilled carbonated water

Spoon ice cream into punch bowl. Stir in eggnog and carbonated water. Top with puffs of cream and sprinkle with candy. Makes 24, ½ cup servings.

EASY HORS D'OEUVRES

If you're entertaining over the holidays consider these easy to make hors d'oeuvres. Ready in a minute they'll please family and friends alike.

Spread bite sized shredded wheat on a cookie sheet. Sprinkle with onion or garlic salt. Broil.

Spread potato chips on a cookie sheet. Sprinkle with grated cheese and onion salt. Broil until bubbly.

Sprinkle parmesan cheese over hot popcorn.

Spread any cheese on saltines, sprinkle with any seasoned salt and paprika. Broil.

Vegetable dip: Make the day before using.
Mix half sour cream and half mayonnaise. Add grated onion, worcestershire, dry mustard, chives, horseradish, salt and black pepper.

MRS. WILLIAM M. BURRIS, JR.

CHICKEN LIVER HORS D'OEUVRES

A simple hors d'oeuvres that can be prepared weeks ahead and frozen.

chicken livers (2-3 per person)
bacon (½ strip per liver)
Reese's Sweet'n Tart Sauce

Variation: May use pineapple chunks or water chestnuts in place of chicken livers.

Wrap each liver with bacon and secure with toothpick. Place on broiler pan. Broil on each side until brown. Serve with sauce for dipping.

MRS. JAMES N. GRANT

MINI QUICHE HORS D'OEUVRES

These little delicacies can be made in advance and frozen. This recipe makes 24 muffin size tarts.

1 pkg. refrigerated butterflake
  dinner rolls
1 4½ oz. can shrimp, drained
1 beaten egg
½ c. light cream

1 T. brandy
½ tsp. salt
dash of pepper
1⅓ oz. gruyère or Swiss cheese

Preheat oven to 375°. Grease 2 dozen 1¾" muffin tins. Separate each dinner roll in half and press into muffin pans to make shell. Place 1 shrimp in each shell. Combine egg, cream, brandy, salt and pepper. Divide evenly among shells, using about 2 tsp. for each. Slice the gruyere into 24 small triangles; place atop each appetizer. Bake for 20 minutes or until golden. Cool. Wrap in foil and freeze. To serve place frozen appetizers on baking sheet and put in 375° oven for 10-12 minutes.

HOT MUSHROOM SANDWICHES

These delightful sandwiches can be frozen ahead and served on a moment's notice.

½ lb. fresh mushrooms
¼ cup butter
3 T. flour
¾ tsp. salt
1 cup light cream (½ and ½)

2 tsp. minced chives
1 tsp. lemon juice
2-3 loaves fresh, white bread,
(crusted and rolled flat)

Clean and chop mushrooms fine. Saute 5 minutes in butter. Blend in flour and salt. Stir in cream and cook until thick. Add 2 tsp. minced chives and lemon juice. Cool. Remove crusts from slices of bread. Roll thin. Spread with mixture. Roll like jelly roll. Place each rolled piece of bread closely together on cookie sheet and freeze. When frozen, remove from sheet and store in plastic bags in freezer. To serve: Thaw. Bake uncovered, toasting on all sides for 7 minutes at 400°.

Variation: Add 1 lb. lobster meat, minced.

MRS. DICK MAXWELL

DEVILED HAM PUFFS

Freeze on cookie sheet, and then place in freezer container — will keep indefinitely.

1 egg yolk
4 oz. cream cheese
1 tsp. onion juice
½ tsp. baking powder

dash salt
24 small bread rounds
2-2¼ oz. cans deviled ham

Preheat oven to 375°. Blend together cheese, onion juice, baking powder, egg yolk and salt. Toast bread rounds on one side. Spread untoasted sides with deviled ham. Cover each with a mound of cream cheese mixture. Bake for 10-12 minutes.

MRS. ROBERT LAWRENCE

HOT CLAM DIP

Possibly the only dip recipe you will ever need. Served hot in a chafing dish it goes with chips, crackers, or vegetables.

2 large pkg. cream cheese
½ stick butter
2 cans minced clams

juice of one lemon
dash of celery salt
dash of seasoning salt
dash of garlic powder

Melt cheese and butter in double boiler. Add clams and seasonings. If too thick, thin with clam juice. Serve hot.

MRS. VANCE W. BRABHAM, III

CHEESE CUBES

A do ahead, freezable hors d'oeuvre. Keep some on hand for all those holiday happenings.

½ lb. grated sharp cheddar
   cheese
½ lb. grated butter

1 slightly beaten egg
1-2 dashes red/cayenne pepper
bread

Preheat oven 350°. Mix first four ingredients together. Decrust 3 slices of bread. Spread mixture on two of the slices and stack placing third slice on top. Make nine cubes out of the stack of bread. Ice 4 sides and top with the mixture. Continue making three slice stacks until you have used all the mixture. Freeze or bake immediately for 12-18 minutes.

MRS. WIMBERLY A. SMITH

COCKTAIL FRANKS

A super simple cocktail treat! Serves about 16.

Small jar burgundy or currant
   jelly

Very small jar mustard
1 pkg. hot dogs

Combine and melt jelly and mustard. Add one package small diameter hot dogs cut in bite size pieces. Add to jelly and heat thoroughly.

DORIS BRAY

CRAB MEAT DIP

2-6 oz. pkg. frozen King Crab
   meat
3-8 oz. pkg. cream cheese
½ cup mayonnaise
½ cup white wine

2 tsp. onion powder
2 tsp. dry mustard
2 tsp. powdered sugar
dash garlic salt

Soften cream cheese in double boiler; add everything but crab meat. Put thawed crab meat, including juice, in chafing dish. Pour hot mixture over meat and stir. Serve with crackers.

MRS. RICHARD WILLIS

BROCCOLI DIP

This is a great recipe to have for parties! It serves 20-30 and can be frozen. Serve hot in chafing dish with Fritoes or Doritoes.

2 rolls garlic cheese
2 pkgs. chopped broccoli
1 large onion (chopped)
4 T. butter

1 small can chopped mushrooms
1 can golden mushroom soup
red pepper and salt

Cook broccoli according to package directions. Drain well. Sauté onions in butter. Place mixture ·and broccoli in double boiler. Add garlic cheese, mushrooms, and soup. Mix well. Add salt and pepper to taste. Cook until melted.

MRS. JOHN W. BLACK

ELEGANT CAVIAR SPREAD

Perfect at Christmas, for when this spread is unmolded, it's red and white. Garnish with parsley and lemons or holly leaves. It goes a long way, serving 24.

1 T. worcestershire sauce
1 T. unflavored gelatin
2 T. cold water
½ cup boiling water
1 T. lemon juice

2 T. mayonnaise
½ pint sour cream
4 oz. whipped cream cheese
2-4 oz. jars red caviar

Soften gelatin in cold water and then dissolve it in the boiling water. Add lemon juice and worcestershire sauce. Blend well. In another bowl, blend the mayonnaise, sour cream and cream cheese. Quickly stir in the gelatin. Add the caviar and pour mixture into a four cup mold and chill until set. Unmold and serve with Melba toast rounds.

MRS. ADAIR M. GRAHAM

EASY CAVIAR CHEESE SPREAD

Using lumpfish, instead of your more expensive caviar, gives the same effect at considerably less cost.

1-8 oz. pkg. cream cheese
   (softened and whipped)
1 T. grated onion or onion to
   taste

⅓ cup mayonnaise
1 container caviar (red for
   Christmas)

Combine cheese, onion, and mayonnaise. Put in small "Cool Whip" container lined with plastic wrap. Chill. Unmold and ice with caviar.

MRS. THOMAS R. HABER, PRINCETON, N.J.

SHRIMP BALL

You can't find an easier spread to make and you know your guests will love it, since it's filled with shrimp.

1 lb. boiled shrimp	8 oz. cream cheese (softened)
½ small onion minced	¼ tsp. garlic powder
1 dash worcestershire	¼ tsp. salt
2 T. mayonnaise	chopped parsley
juice of ½ lemon	paprika

Mix all ingredients together by hand. Form into ball. Sprinkle with parsley and paprika. Serve with crackers.

MRS. TED A. STURM

SARDINE BALL

An easy spread perfect during the holiday rush. Do a day ahead.

1 T. mayonnaise	1 T. chopped onion
2 cans sardines	1 tsp. vinegar
1 T. hot horseradish	1 tsp. sherry
1 T. mustard	

Open sardines and remove bones. Mash. Combine with remaining ingredients. Shape into ball and chill thoroughly. Serve with crackers.

SPINACH SPREAD

This spread can be served as an hors d'oeuvre on crackers or as a garnish with meal.

1 box frozen chopped spinach	1 T. mayonnaise
2 or 3 spring onions, (finely chopped)	(optional — sour cream, salt, and pepper)

Thaw spinach, drain well. Stir in onions and mayonnaise. Add optional ingredients to taste at this point.

MRS. C. A. MATTHEWS

GIN SPREAD

This spicy spread keeps up to 2 weeks in the refrigerator. Great on Triscuits!

2-3 oz. Philadelphia Cream Cheese	1 shallot, chopped
¼ cup butter	½ tsp. caraway seeds
1 tsp. capers, chopped	½ tsp. salt
1 tsp. paprika	1 tsp. minced green pepper
2 anchovies, chopped	2 to 3 T. gin

Combine ingredients and mix well. Refrigerate 24 hours before serving.

MERLE M. NOLAND

CURRY DIP

A new twist for your vegetable tray that can be made a day or two ahead.

1 container (4 oz.) whipped cream cheese with chives	1 tsp. curry powder
¼ cup sour cream	¼ tsp. salt

Mix all ingredients together and chill.

MRS. JAMES ABERNATHY

CHILI-CHEESE LOG

Great to have on hand ready for party entertaining. Easy to fix the day before needed, or freeze and keep indefinitely.

1-8 oz. pkg. cream cheese	dash red pepper
2 cups shredded sharp process American cheese (8 oz.)	¼ cup finely chopped pecans
1 T. lemon juice	1 tsp. chili powder
¼ tsp. garlic powder	1 tsp. paprika

Let cheese stand at room temperature to soften. Mix first five ingredients with electric mixer or rotary beater until light and fluffy. Stir in nuts. Place in refrigerator a few minutes to let cheese get firmer. (Easier to handle and shape into logs if cheeses are not too soft.) Shape in log 1½" in diameter. Sprinkle with mixture of chili powder and paprika. Chill. Let stand at room temperature for 10 minutes before serving. Serve with crackers.

MRS. HARRY H. CLENDENIN, III

MARINATED PARTY SHRIMP

A party favorite that can be put together the day before. May be served as entree or hors d'oeuvre.

3 lbs. cooked shrimp (fresh or frozen)
2 cans whole mushrooms (3½ oz.) or 1 lb. fresh
3 onions (medium) sliced and ringed

dash pepper	1 bay leaf
¾ cup salad oil	1 tsp. worcestershire sauce
1 cup vinegar	1 tsp. Tobasco
2 tsp. salt	

Layer shrimp, mushrooms and onions in large bowl with a tight-fitting cover. Pour marinade over all. Cover and refrigerate for 24 hours. Stir occasionally. Drain and serve. Serves 20.

MRS. JACK UPTON

LEG OF LAMB

salt and pepper	3 T. worcestershire sauce
2 cloves garlic	rosemary leaves
flour	juice of ½ lemon
¾ cup catsup	

Preheat oven 475°. Rub lamb with garlic, then salt and pepper. Sprinkle with flour. Combine remaining ingredients to form sauce and pour over lamb. Brown for 15 minutes. Reduce oven to 350° and cook 1½ hours or until done.

MRS. BRUCE CAMERON, WILMINGTON, N.C.

BOEUF BOURGUIGNON

This recipe can be made in a crock pot or cooked over very low heat for almost an entire day allowing you time to do all your other holiday chores. This recipe serves 10 people.

¾ lb. sirloin tip per person	4 T. flour
4 lbs. onion (sliced)	2 T. salt
stick of butter	½ of a fifth of Burgundy wine
1 T. thyme	2 lbs. mushrooms (sliced)
1 T. marjoram	

Cut meat into 1½ to 2 inch cubes or have your butcher do it. In large frying pan melt butter and brown meat. Place meat in Dutch oven or crock pot. Glaze onions in remaining grease in frying pan. Add flour, salt, and spices. Add to meat. Pour about 1 cup of wine over mixture then continue drizzling wine over mixture throughout the day. About 1 hour before serving saute mushrooms and add to meat. Serve over non-sticky rice (p. 51).

MRS. RALPH FAIRBANKS, PRINCETON, N.J.

HAM AND VEAL MEAT LOAF

This economical recipe for meat loaf adds a new dimension to an old favorite. The peach syrup glaze and peach garnish make it especially festive.

1 cup bread (broken in bits)	large can peach halves
1 cup milk	2 T. vinegar
2 eggs	1½ cups brown sugar
1 lb. ham (ground)	
1 lb. veal (ground)	

Preheat oven to 350°. Have ready standard sized roaster pan. Soak bread in milk. Add beaten eggs and milk to meats. Form into loaf. Drain juice from large can of peach halves into sauce pan. Add vinegar and brown sugar, and bring mixture to a boil. Dot meat loaf with whole cloves. Put in roaster. Pour liquid over top. Bake 1½ hours. Baste occasionally. When ½ done, place peach halves around meat.

NEW YEAR'S CHICKEN

This special chicken casserole is loved by men. It will become a necessity around your house during the holidays. Serves 12.

3½ cups chicken or turkey
1 lb. pkg. hot sausage
1-6 oz. box Uncle Ben's long
   grain and wild rice with
   seasonings

2 to 2½ cups chicken broth
2 cans mushroom soup
   (undiluted)
1 cup herb stuffing mix
1 T. melted butter

Cut up chicken into small pieces. Scramble sausage in frying pan. Follow directions on rice package for preparation of rice, using broth instead of water. Stir all ingredients together in bowl and put in a 7½" x 12" Pyrex casserole dish. Sprinkle with herb stuffing mix that has been tossed with a tablespoon of melted butter. Bake 350° for 30 minutes.

MRS. VAN WOLTZ

CHICKEN BROCCOLI CASSEROLE

For a delicious entrée or luncheon dish make this casserole a day in advance or weeks in advance and freeze. Substitute turkey for chicken after the big Christmas feast. Serves 6-8.

1 pkg. frozen broccoli (cooked
   and cut in pieces)
8 chicken breasts or 1 stewing
   hen (cooked and cut in pieces)
1 can cream of chicken soup

½ cup mayonnaise
2 T. lemon juice
¼ tsp. curry powder
Pepperidge Farm Dressing

Preheat oven 350°. Combine soup, mayonnaise, juice and curry powder. Season to taste. Layer broccoli, chicken and soup mixture in a 1 quart casserole. Top with good layer of dressing crumbs. Heat 30-40 minutes. Topping browns quickly but be sure to heat through.

MRS. HERBERT OWEN DAVIS

CHICKEN CASSEROLE

An easy, do ahead recipe that can be reheated when ready to serve.

½ 8 oz. pkg. noodles cooked and
   drained
½ cup mayonnaise
1 green pepper, chopped
1 medium yellow onion (chopped)

1 cup chopped celery
1½ cups milk
1 can cream of mushroom soup
½ cup grated sharp cheese
2 cups cooked
   chicken, chopped

Preheat oven to 350°. Grease casserole dish. Mix together all ingredients and pour over cooked and drained noodles. Cover casserole with foil or lid. Bake 30 minutes.

MRS. ALAN SUTTON

CHICKEN SPAGHETTI

This recipe is great for company, gift giving, or planning ahead for family meals during the holidays. It makes 2 2-quart casseroles which can be frozen.

1-5 lb. chicken	1-4 oz. can mushrooms
1 cup butter or margarine	1-3 oz. can tomato paste
¾ cup all purpose flour	1-4 oz. can pimientos (cut fine)
5 cups chicken broth	2 small cloves garlic (minced)
1 cup milk	1 cup sliced green olives
1 cup chopped celery	1-8 oz. package spaghetti

Cover chicken with water and cook until meat begins to come off bones. Remove from broth and cool, then cut into small pieces. Measure 4½ cups broth and set aside. Melt butter; add flour and stir until dissolved. Add chicken broth and milk. Cook until mixture is thick. Add celery, mushrooms, tomato paste, pimientos, garlic, olives and cooked chicken. Let stand about an hour. Cook spaghetti according to package directions. Combine spaghetti and chicken mixture. Put into two (2 quart) baking dishes; cover with foil or put into plastic bags. Seal securely and freeze. To serve, remove from freezer and let stand overnight in refrigerator. Bake 350° for 30 or 40 minutes.

DEGAS DISH

You'll find this Mexican sounding dish to be a super spaghetti type casserole. The sauce is much better if made a day in advance and refrigerated. It can be frozen so is perfect for holidays. Serves 10.

1 medium onion	4 oz. can sliced mushrooms
1 lb. ground beef	4 oz. bottle stuffed olives sliced
15 oz. can tomato sauce	1 small jar pimientos (chopped)
15 oz. can tomatoes	12 oz. package spaghetti
¾ cup tomato catsup	1 cup grated cheese
dash of Tobasco	1½ tsp. salt
dash of Worcestershire	⅛ tsp. pepper

Preheat oven 350°. Using a large deep skillet cook onion in a small amount of oil until golden. Add beef and cook slowly until lightly browned. Drain off fat. Add tomato sauce, tomatoes, catsup, Tabasco, Worcestershire, salt and pepper. Cook slowly for several hours until cooked down and thick like a spaghetti sauce. Add mushrooms, olives, pimientos. Cook spaghetti according to package directions. Drain and add to heated sauce and mix thoroughly. Put mixture in shallow pyrex casserole and cover with cheese. Bake 20 minutes.

MRS. JOHN W. BLACK

TOMATO PEAR CHOPS

This recipe is an easy, tasty preparation for an economical cut of meat. Nice for company.

8 lean pork chops	bread crumbs
2-1 lb. cans pears (save juice)	garlic salt
4 tomatoes (cut in half)	salt and pepper, to taste
mayonnaise	½ cup water
poultry seasoning	

Preheat oven 350°. Place pork chops, tomatoes, and pears in baking dish. Put 1 tsp. mayonnaise in center of pears. Shake poultry seasoning and garlic salt generously over chop combination. Salt and pepper to taste. Cover with bread crumbs. Add ½ cup water to pear juice, pour over everything and bake 1-1¼ hours. Serves 4-6.

MRS. TED A. STURM

MOTHER'S SCALLOPED OYSTERS

Here's an easy, last minute dish that is a must for your holiday table.

1 cup dry bread crumbs	salt
2 cups cracker crumbs	pepper
1 cup melted butter	4 T. oyster liquor
1 quart oysters	4 T. cream

Preheat oven to 400-450 degrees. Butter a shallow baking dish. Mix bread and cracker crumbs together. Stir crumbs in butter. Put ⅓ of crumb mixture in bottom of baking dish. Cover with ½ of the oysters. Sprinkle with salt and pepper. Add ½ each of oyster liquor and cream. Repeat. Cover top with remaining crumbs. Bake 30 minutes. Serves 8.

MRS. HOWARD SPROCK

WILD RICE AND SHRIMP CASSEROLE

This dish is great for buffet style entertainment because it is elegant yet does not require the use of a knife for eating. It serves 8-10. To stretch the recipe, use another box of wild rice and slice shrimp in half lengthwise.

2 pkg. Uncle Ben's Wild Rice (do not use seasoning)	½ cup dry white wine
	½ tsp. salt
4 T. butter or margarine	¼ tsp. garlic salt
1 onion (finely chopped)	¼ tsp. crumbled dried tarragon
1 lb. medium mushrooms	3 T. grated Parmesan Cheese
Juice of ½ lemon	1 lb. cooked medium shrimp (shelled and deveined)
2 T. flour	
1¼ cup chicken stock	1 pkg. King Crab (6 oz.)
1 T. chopped parsley	

Preheat oven to 350°. Cook rice according to directions on the box until almost tender. Meanwhile, melt 2 T. of butter in large frying pan, add onion and saute until golden. Wash mushrooms, slice stems off leaving caps whole. Add mushroom caps and stems to pan and sprinkle with lemon juice. Cook gently, stirring occasionally until tender. In another pan melt 2 T. butter and blend flour mixing to make a roux. Pour in the chicken stock and wine; cook stirring constantly until thickened. Season with salt, garlic salt and tarragon. Stir in Parmesan cheese. Mix together ¾ of sauce, wild rice, mushrooms and seafood, reserving a few shrimp and crab pieces for garnish. Spoon into 2 qt. casserole. Garnish with extra seafood and spoon over the remaining sauce. (If making ahead, refrigerate at this point). Cover and bake 45 minutes to an hour. Sprinkle with parsley before serving.

MRS. JAMES M. DOWTIN, JR.

CLAM BISQUE

1 large chopped onion	2-8 oz. bottles clam juice
6 T. butter	3 cups light table cream
6 T. flour	3 T. tomato paste
3-8 oz. cans minced clams	3 T. lemon juice

Combine cream, tomato paste, and lemon juice and set aside. Saute onion in butter until soft in large (3 qt.) saucepan. Stir in flour, and stir constantly until bubbly. Add clams and juice, and continue cooking until mixture thickens and boils for 1 minute. Reduce heat, cover and simmer for 15 minutes. Then blend in cream mixture until heated. Can be frozen or kept in refrigerator. When reheating — heat slowly, do not boil.

MRS. SCOTT LACY

FLORINE'S POTATO SOUP

This winter-time specialty is better if made a day in advance. Serves 6-8.

2½ cups cold water	1 T. butter
2 cups cooked diced ham	½ tsp. parsley flakes
2 cups peeled and diced potatoes	sprinkle heavily with Accent
½ cup chopped onions	¼ tsp. paprika
½ cup diced celery	1 cup milk
2 heaping T. bacon grease	water and flour

Combine all ingredients except paprika and milk. Cook until potatoes are done. Add milk. Thicken with 2 T. flour and a little more water. Cook until it comes to a boil. Turn off heat and add paprika.

MRS. ALAN SUTTON

JENNY'S EGGS

This dish can be frozen, but flavor is even better when made the day before and baked just prior to serving time. Serves 8-10.

15 slices sandwich bread (cubed)	½ lb. butter
1 lb. Velveeta cheese	8 eggs beaten
½ lb. margarine	4 cups milk

Place bread cubes in dish. Melt cheese, margarine, and butter. Pour over bread. Mix eggs and milk. Pour egg and milk mixture over above and refrigerate over night. When ready to serve, bake at 300° in 9 x 13 inch pyrex dish for 1 hour. Keep warm on a hot tray.

MRS. THOMAS R. BEARD

QUICHE

3 eggs slightly beaten	1-3½ oz. can French fried
1 cup sour cream	onion rings
¾ tsp. salt	8 slices crumbled bacon
½ tsp. worcestershire sauce	1 baked 9 inch pie shell
1 cup (¼ lb.) Swiss cheese, grated	

Preheat oven 350°. Combine first six ingredients. Pour in pie shell and crumble bacon on top. Bake ½ hour.

MRS. JOHN W. BLACK

MANDY'S CHEESE SOUFFLE

This fake cheese soufflé will be a great recipe to have on hand during the busy holidays.

1 cup sharp grated cheese	2 eggs
6 slices of bread	1 cup milk
½ stick butter or more, (melted)	

Make 3 sandwiches with cheese (thick). Dip sandwiches in butter on both sides. Cut sandwiches into 9 squares and put in 9"x9" casserole. Beat eggs and milk thoroughly — pour over sandwiches and let stand 30 to 40 minutes. Bake until a "pretty" brown, about 20 minutes at 400°.

MRS. FRANK HANCOCK

ANGELS ON HORSEBACK

For each open faced sandwich use the following ingredients:

1 slice (decrusted) bread	1 slice cheese
mayonnaise	1 slice onion (optional)
1 slice tomato (optional)	1 slice bacon

Spread mayonnaise on bread. Then layer ingredients in order given to suit the taste of your guest. Broil slowly until bacon browns.

APRICOT CONGEALED SALAD

2-3 oz. pkg. apricot gelatin
1½ cup boiling water
1-6 oz. can frozen orange juice, undiluted
2 T. lemon juice

1-7 oz. bottle Sprite or Fresca
1 can junior baby apricots
dash of salt
1 small can crushed pineapple
chopped nuts

Dissolve gelatin in 1½ cups boiling water. Add all other ingredients. Congeal. Serves 12.

MRS. CHARLES ALLEN, HENDERSONVILLE, N.C.

RASPBERRY CONGEALED SALAD

As a gift — deliver in mold or on plate with sour cream/marshmallow topping. Looks like Christmas!

1 carton (½ pt.) sour cream
1-15 oz. can apple sauce
1 pkg. raspberry Jello

1 cup small marshmallows
1 cup raspberries (frozen)

Heat apple sauce over medium heat. Add Jello and raspberries; then pour into a mold and chill. Mix sour cream and marshmallows together and add to top. Serves 6-8.

MRS. A. B. McLEAN

STRAWBERRY CONGEALED SALAD

This salad is very Christmasy and very rich. Serves 8.

2 pkg. strawberry Jello
1 envelope plain gelatin
2 bananas

1 small can crushed pineapple
1 small pkg. frozen strawberries
1-8 oz. carton sour cream

Thaw strawberries. Dissolve 2 packages jello in 2 cups boiling water. Add 1 envelope plain gelatin mixed with small amount of water. Mix together: 2 mashed bananas, crushed pineapple, strawberries. After jello has cooled add fruit. Pour ½ of mixture into a bowl and congeal remainder in a 6″x10″ casserole dish. When completely congealed, spread sour cream on top. Pour other half of jello-fruit mixture on top. Congeal.

CONGEALED BROCCOLI SALAD

A new twist for one of the most popular vegetables. Easy to prepare and can be done one or two days in advance to serve 8-12.

2 packages frozen chopped broccoli
4 hard boiled eggs
2 envelopes gelatin
¼ cup cold water
1 can consommé

¾ cup mayonnaise
1¾ tsp. salt
2 tsp. lemon juice
4 tsp. worcestershire
dash of Tobasco

Cook broccoli until tender. Drain well. Chop eggs coarsely. Soften gelatin in cold water and add to heated consommé. Stir until dissolved. Mix with broccoli and eggs. Combine mayonnaise, salt, lemon juice, worcestershire and Tobasco. Fold into consommé mixture. Turn into mold and refrigerate.

ASPARAGUS SALAD

1 cup boiling water	½ cup sharp grated cheese
1 pkg. lime Jello	1 T. onion juice
¼ cup asparagus juice	1 T. vinegar
¼ tsp. salt	dash of red pepper
1 cup mayonnaise	1 can chopped, tender green
½ cup milk	asparagus

Dissolve lime Jello in 1 cup boiling water. Add ¼ cup asparagus juice and ¼ tsp. salt. Set aside to chill. Gradually mix together 1 cup mayonnaise and ½ cup milk. When smooth add ¼ cup grated cheese, 1 T. onion juice, 1 T. vinegar and dash of red pepper. Add all this to cooled Jello. Then add 1 can chopped asparagus. Mix and chill until set.

MRS. TED A. STURM

WATERCRESS AND ORANGE SALAD

This tart salad is a compliment to most seafood dishes. Salad greens may be prepared in the morning but do not put dressing on until serving time. Serves 6-8.

2 bunches curly endive	½ cup vegetable oil
2 bunches watercress	4 T. lemon juice
4 oranges peeled and sectioned	1 tsp. sugar or to taste
4 shallots finely chopped	salt and coarsely ground black
½ cup olive oil	pepper

Wash endive and break in small pieces. Wash watercress and trim off stems. Combine in large bowl. Top with orange sections before serving. To make dressing combine shallots, oils, lemon juice and sugar. Add salt and pepper to taste. Blend well with fork. Pour over greens and toss well.

MRS. JAMES M. DOWTIN, JR.

PEA SALAD

This is an excellent dish men seem to love, believe it or not. Must be done 12 hours ahead.

½ head lettuce	1 pint Hellman's mayonnaise
1 small red onion	3 T. sugar
5 stalks celery	1-3 oz. container Parmesan cheese
2 cans green peas, (8½ oz.)	1 box real bacon bits

Chop lettuce into large pieces. Chop onion and celery into small pieces. Drain peas. Mix these ingredients together. Spread sugar mixed with mayonnaise over above mixture. Sprinkle cheese and crumbled bacon bits over the entire mixture. Chill 12 hours.

MRS. JOHN E. BARNEY

MARINATED ARTICHOKES

Though easy to prepare, this is a very special appetizer. May want to substitute olives for artichokes some time.

canned artichokes	2 cloves garlic, sliced
olice oil (good variety)	2-3 T. chopped chives
spicy vinegar	2-3 T. parsley
capers	

Drain artichokes and cover with half oil, half vinegar. Add remaining ingredients. Cover and refrigerate. Will keep for days.

MRS. JOHN T. GREGORY

BROILED PEACHES

This peach dish is an attractive compliment to almost any meal when arranged on platter with parsley sprigs.

1-29 oz. can of peach halves	ground nutmeg
butter	ground cloves

On broiler pan (or square pyrex or aluminum pan) arrange drained peach halves, cut side up. Dot each with a pat of butter, and sprinkle lightly with nutmeg and cloves. Broil 4 to 5 minutes or until browned.

MRS. DICK WILLIS

SPINACH SOUFFLE STUFFED TOMATOES

Your guests will think you spent hours concocting this impressive dish, but it only takes about fifteen minutes. A colorful accent to any meal but especially great at Christmas.

4 firm, medium tomatoes
1 pkg. Stouffer's Spinach Soufflé

Earlier in the day cut off tops of tomatoes and scoop out insides. Salt lightly and turn upside down on paper towels to drain. Defrost spinach soufflé until "spoonable." Spoon into tomatoes. Cook 45 min. to 1 hour, or until soufflé is puffy and slightly browned. Do not overcook because tomatoes will lose their shape.

MRS. JAMES M. DOWTIN, JR.

SPINACH AND ARTICHOKE CASSEROLE

3 pkg. frozen chopped spinach
1-8 oz. pkg. cream cheese
1 can artichoke hearts

Parmesan cheese
1 stick of butter
cracker crumbs

Preheat oven to 350°. Mix cream cheese and butter. Cook spinach, drain, and mix with cream cheese and butter. Put in soufflé dish. Drain artichoke hearts and slice in quarters. Press artichokes in under spinach. Sprinkle top with layer of cracker crumbs and Parmesan cheese. Bake 30 minutes.

MRS. PHILLIP HERVEY

BURGUNDY BEETS

1-11 oz. can mandarin orange
sections
½ cup Burgundy wine

4 tsp. cornstarch
1 tsp. lemon juice
1 can (16 oz.) beets — tiny, whole

Drain orange sections and reserve liquid. In sauce pan, combine liquid, wine and cornstarch. Bring to boil, stirring constantly. Add lemon juice, beets and orange sections. Heat through, stirring gently. Serves 4-6.

PAT STAPLETON

CORN AND BEAN CASSEROLE

1 pkg. frozen white shoepeg corn,
partially cooked
1 pkg. frozen French green
beans, partially cooked
½ cup bean juice reserved from
cooking

¾ cup broken pecans
⅔ cup grated cheese
1½ cups cracker crumbs
½ cup melted butter

In large casserole, place in alternating layers ½ beans, ½ corn, and ½ pecans. Pour bean juice over top. Sprinkle top with cheese and crumbs. Pour butter over all. Bake at 350° for 30 minutes.

MRS. ROBERT H. BORDEN

BLEU CHEESE AND BACON POTATOES

20 small new red potatoes
½ lb. bacon
1 cup mayonnaise

¼ cup whipping cream
(slightly whipped)
¼ cup Roquefort cheese
finely chopped parsley

Boil potatoes until tender. Fry, drain and crumble bacon. Combine mayonnaise, cream and Roquefort cheese. Fold dressing into whole or sliced potatoes. Garnish with crumbled bacon and parsley.

MRS. OTIS N. FISHER

POTATO SOUFFLÉ

A pleasant diversion for your meat and potato lovers. Serves 6-8.

1-8 oz. cream cheese, softened
4 cups hot mashed potatoes
1 egg beaten

⅓ cup finely chopped pimiento
1 tsp. salt
dash pepper

Preheat oven 350°. Combine cream cheese and potatoes, mixing well until well blended. Add remaining ingredients. Place in 1-qt. casserole. Bake 45 minutes.

MRS. JOHN T. GREGORY

BROWN RICE

1 cup raw rice
3 T. butter

1 can beef bouillon (undiluted)
1 can onion soup (undiluted)

Fry rice in butter, stirring constantly until golden brown. Add soups. Pour into greased casserole. Bake at 350° for 45 minutes. (May take longer for liquid to absorb).

MRS. JAMES ABERNATHY

NON-STICKY RICE

This rice will be very fluffy. Much better than minute rice and really no trouble.

1 tsp. salt

1 cup Uncle Ben's rice

Fill 2 qt. container almost full of water. Add salt and let come to full boil. Add rice and cook about 20 minutes. Put in collander and pour cold water through until well rinsed. Place in inch deep pyrex dish and place on top shelf of 400° oven for about ten minutes.

MRS. BEVERLY C. MOORE

HOMEMADE ROLLS

To many there is no bigger treat than freshly baked homemade bread. These rolls are special because the dough can be kept in a tupperware container in your refrigerator for weeks. Simply punch off what you need for each meal. Makes 5 dozen.

3 T. baking powder
1½ pkg. yeast   1 tsp. baking soda
2 T. water   1½ tsp. salt
2 cups buttermilk   ¼ cup sugar
5 cups sifted flour   ¾ cup Crisco

Sift together flour, sugar, baking soda, powder and salt. Cut in shortening. Meanwhile dissolve yeast into 2 T. warm water. Add buttermilk. Combine with flour mixture. Turn out on lightly floured board and knead 5-10 minutes. If necessary add additional flour to make a soft dough. Make into favorite roll shape (parkerhouse, clover leaf, etc.). Brush top with butter. Let rise 3-5 hours. Place rolls on buttered pan. Preheat oven 400°. Cook on low rack for 10 minutes, then move to higher rack for five additional minutes.

MRS. VANCE W. BRABHAM, III

ORANGE MUFFINS

½ cup shortening   2 cups flour
1 cup sugar   1 tsp. salt
2 eggs, beaten   ⅔ cup buttermilk
1 tsp. soda
Uncooked Icing:
    1½ cups orange juice   grated rind of 4 oranges
    ¾ cup sugar

Preheat oven to 375°. Cream sugar and shortening. Add eggs one at a time; beat. Combine dry ingredients and add alternately with buttermilk. Fill very small, greased muffin tins ½ full (about 1 tsp.). After cooking remove from pans. Combine icing ingredients and pour over muffins while still warm.

MRS. THOMAS R. BEARD

BEER MUFFINS

An unique accompaniment to those suppers by the fire. Serves 8.

2 cups Bisquick   1 cup beer
2 T. sugar

Preheat oven 400°. Combine Bisquick, sugar and beer. Let rise 15-20 minutes. Put in greased muffin tins. Bake for 10 minutes.

MRS. HOYT BROWN

RUM PUDDING

This is a very rich dessert and can be made up to 2 days ahead. Serves 10.

2 egg yolks
½ cup powdered sugar
2 egg whites
2 T. Meyer's Dark Rum

1 pt. heavy cream
1 doz. double crushed macaroons
½ doz. lady fingers

Beat yolks of 2 eggs with ½ cup powdered sugar. Beat whites separately; then add, beating constantly, to egg yolks and sugar. Add rum. Whip one pint heavy cream and fold into mixture; add crushed macaroons. Line mold or ice trays with lady fingers. Keep in freezer.

MRS. EDWIN S. MELVIN

YULETIDE CHOCOLATE DESSERT

A delicious and unique holiday treat. Must be made at least 24 hours before serving or can be frozen. Perfect for the hostess that likes to do things ahead. Serves 9. Use square 8" x 8" or 9" x 9" pan.

2 cups fine vanilla wafer crumbs
⅓ cup melted butter
½ cup butter
1½ cups powdered sugar
2 eggs
¼ cup sugar

2 T. cocoa
1 cup heavy cream
1 cup chopped walnuts
1-2 fully ripe bananas (mashed)
½ cup sliced maraschino
    cherries

Mix together crumbs and melted butter in pan. Put aside 2 T. for topping. Press the remainder into bottom of pan. Cream together ½ cup butter and powdered sugar. Add eggs, one at a time, beating well after each. Spread over crumbs. Combine sugar, cocoa, cream; whip. Fold in nuts and fruits. Pile atop mixture in pan. Sprinkle reserved crumbs over dessert. Chill 24 hours or freeze, then allow to thaw 15 minutes before serving. The frozen way tastes best.

MRS. OTIS N. FISHER

TEXAS CHRISTMAS PUDDING

This easy, yet unique, Christmas pudding can be frozen ahead of time.

4 egg yolks
½ cup sugar
½ cup sweet rosé wine or brandy
4 egg whites
green food coloring

½ box crystalized mixed fruit
    (pineapple, cherries, etc.)
1 cup pecans (cut up fine)
1 pt. whipping cream

Cook egg yolks, sugar and wine over low heat in double boiler until thick; cool. Beat 4 egg whites until stiff and fold into mixture. Add crystalized fruit and nuts to mixture. Beat cream until stiff. Add green coloring to make a pale green and fold into mixture. Put in a Pyrex dish and refrigerate. Freeze if not used immediately.

MRS. JOHN ELLISON

PECAN TARTS

Yummy "finger-desserts," perfect for buffet entertaining.

Crust:

> 1 stick margarine or butter   1 cup flour
> 3 oz. cream cheese

Using double boiler melt butter with cream cheese. Add this to 1 cup flour and knead well. (May chill here for easier handling.) Divide into 24 small balls. Using fingers press into small cup muffin tins.

Filling:

> ¾ cup brown sugar   1 tsp. vanilla
> 1 egg beaten   ¾ cup pecans
> 1 T. melted butter or margarine

Preheat oven 350°. Combine filling ingredients in saucepan and heat for five minutes. Fill muffin tins. Bake 20 minutes.

NOEL BARS

Decorative as well as good, men even like these nutty bars! If you don't have time to write "Noel" on each bar simply sprinkle with powdered sugar.

> 2 T. butter   1 cup chopped nuts
> ⅓ cup flour   2 beaten eggs
> ⅛ tsp. baking soda   1 tsp. vanilla
> ⅛ tsp. salt   powdered sugar
> 1 cup brown sugar

Preheat oven 350°. Melt butter in 9 x 9 x 2 pan. Combine flour, salt, and soda in a bowl. Stir in sugar and nuts followed by eggs and vanilla. Carefully pour batter over butter in pan. DO NOT STIR! Bake 20-25 minutes. Sprinkle with sifted powdered sugar. Invert on waxed paper rack immediately. When cool, cut into long bars and write "Noel" in green icing on powdered sugar side.

BARBARA RENTENBACH

BUCKEYES

> 6 cups powdered sugar, sifted   12 oz. pkg. chocolate chips
> 1½ cups peanut butter   ¼ cup melted paraffin
> 1 cup (2 sticks) butter, soft

Mix sugar, peanut butter and butter together with hands. Roll into balls about the size of a strawberry. Melt chocolate chips and paraffin in double boiler. Use toothpicks to dip balls of mixture into the chocolate. Be sure to leave chocolate over hot water while dipping. Recipe makes 175!

MRS. WILLIAM H. WILKERSON

JELLO STRAWBERRIES

For authentic looking strawberries place 2 small leaves (i.e. boxwood) on top of each "strawberry." A lovely accent to any holiday table.

1 tsp. vanilla	
2 pkg. strawberry Jello	pinch of salt
½ can Eagle Brand Milk	red food coloring
2 cups Angel Flake Coconut	sugar (small amount)

Mix Jello (dry) into Eagle Brand Milk. Add coconut, vanilla and salt; let stand several hours or overnight. Form into strawberry shapes and roll into sugar colored red.

OLIVE JORDAN

PECAN SQUARES

When you need an easy, do ahead, finger dessert try these pecan squares. They really keep well, up to two weeks in a tin.

1 cup butter	2 cups flour
1 cup granulated sugar	2 tsp. cinnamon
1 egg (separated)	1 cup chopped pecans

Preheat oven 300°. Cream butter and sugar. Add egg yolk. Sift flour once and then measure 2 cups. Sift again with cinnamon. Add to sugar mixture. Pat mixture evenly on top of greased 12″ x 15″ or 18″ cookie sheet. Brush whipped egg white on mixture. Press pecans into mixture and bake for 20-25 minutes. Cut into squares.

MRS. CHARLES R. BENNETT

AUNT MARY'S CORNFLAKE COOKIES

An uncomplicated recipe that can be put together quickly with things you normally have on hand in your cupboard. Makes 75 cookies.

1 cup (2 sticks) butter or margarine	2 cups flour
1 cup sugar	1 tsp. soda
1 cup brown sugar	1 tsp. salt
2 eggs	1 cup Angel Flake Coconut
1 tsp. vanilla	4 cups cornflakes

Preheat oven to 350°. Grease cookie sheets. Cream butter and sugars. Add eggs and vanilla. Sift dry ingredients together and add to other mixture. Add coconut and cornflakes. Bake 15 minutes.

MRS. ALAN W. SUTTON

SNOWBALLS

A perfect holiday treat especially loved by children without the whipped cream. Put a sprig of holly on top or on the side of the plate for added flair. Makes approximately 12 but the thickness of your filling layers determines number. Will keep several days in the refrigerator.

1 stick butter or margarine	½ box raisins
1 cup sugar	1 box butter cookies
1-No. 2 can crushed pineapple (drained)	1 pint whipping cream (whipped and sweetened to taste)
1 cup chopped nuts	1 cup Angel Flake Coconut

Cream sugar and butter. Add next three ingredients. Layer filling between three cookies. Place on cookie sheet and let stand in refrigerator for 24 hours. Ice each nest of cookies with whipped cream and sprinkle with coconut two to three hours before serving.

MRS. JAMES T. WILLIAMS

HOMEMADE COOKIE MIX

This recipe is a "must" for any time but especially during the holidays. It makes 21 cups of mix that keeps for 6 months or longer when stored in airtight containers. Great for Christmas cookies, sugar cookies, raisin cookies etc.!

1-2 lb. box cake flour plus	1 T. salt
2¼ cups bread flour	8 cups sugar
⅓ cup baking powder	3 cups shortening

Sift dry ingredients 3 times, using two large containers such as a roasting pan. Cut in shortening with mixer at low speed. Store in airtight containers in 3 cup or 6 cup amounts. Stays fresh six months or more. To make cookies: Preheat oven 350°. Use 3 cups mix, 1 egg slightly beaten, ¼ tsp. nutmeg, 1 tsp. vanilla. Refrigerate. Roll out thin, cut out Christmas shapes, decorate and add sugar, and bake on greased pan 5-10 minutes. Roll up scraps, add big raisins, and make big fat raisin cookies. Bake 12 minutes at 350°. Sprinkle sugar over.

For sugar cookies, roll in balls, place on cookie sheet, then mash. Sprinkle sugar over cookies before cooking.

MRS. A. KIRBY MOORE, JR.

FUDGE CUPCAKES

Fabulous cupcakes adults will especially like. Great for luncheon or for tea if you use the miniature muffin tins. Yields 2 doz. of regular sized cupcakes.

1¾ cups sugar	1½ cups chopped pecans
1 cup all-purpose flour	1 tsp. vanilla
4 eggs	4 squares semi-sweet chocolate
1 cup margarine	

Preheat oven to 325°. Combine sugar, flour and eggs, blending by hand. Do not beat. Melt chocolate and margarine in a saucepan. Stir in nuts. Combine sugar mixture, chocolate mixture, and vanilla, blending but not beating. Pour into paper-lined muffin tins. Bake 30 minutes.

DOT BECK

BLACK FOREST CHERRY TORTE

A simple preparation for a fabulous dessert. Make 2-3 days ahead to eliminate last minute rush. Serves 15.

Duncan Hines Devil's Food cake mix	1 can cherry pie filling
1 small bottle rum extract	2 large cartons Cool Whip

Bake the 2 layer cake according to directions on package. Cool and split to make four layers. Sprinkle each layer with rum extract, using ⅔ of bottle. (Do not use real rum as a substitute!) Spread ⅓ of pie filling on three of the layers. Then spread Cool Whip on top of pie filling. Stack layers. Place fourth layer on top. Ice top and sides with Cool Whip. (Will take about a whole container.) Chill thoroughly in large covered Tupperware container.

MRS. JAMES ABERNATHY

HOLLAND ICE BOX CAKE

A rich and elegant do ahead dessert for holiday dinner party. Serves 16.

1 cup butter	2 dozen lady fingers
2 cups confectioner's sugar	½ pt. whipped cream (flavored with sugar and vanilla to taste)
3 eggs (separate yolks and whites)	1 medium sized bottle maraschino cherries
3 squares semi-sweet chocolate	1 cup chopped nuts
1 tsp. vanilla	

Line 2 loaf pans with waxed paper. Cream butter and confectioner's sugar. Add 3 egg yolks and beat well. Melt chocolate and add to above. Add vanilla. Fold in egg whites stiffly beaten. Put lady fingers on sides and bottoms of prepared pans. Pour in chocolate filling. Place in refrigerator for 24 hours. Remove from pan (by lifting out waxed paper) and pile on sweetened whipped cream, nuts, and cherries.

MRS. JAMES E. BETTS

SOUR CREAM COFFEE CAKE

*This is a fabulous variation of the ever popular sour cream coffee cake.
The raisins make the difference. Can be made in bundt pan or two loaf pans
and be frozen indefinitely.*

2 cups flour	2 eggs
1 tsp. baking powder	1 cup sour cream
¼ tsp. salt	½ tsp. vanilla
1 tsp. cinnamon	½ c. white raisins
2 cups sugar	1 cup chopped nuts
1 cup butter (room temp.)	

Preheat oven 350°. Combine first four ingredients and set aside. Cream
butter and sugar til light and fluffy. Beat in eggs, one at a time. Mix in
sour cream and vanilla. Add dry ingredients in thirds mixing well after each
addition. Stir in raisins and ¾ cup of nuts. Pour batter into well greased
bundt pan. Sprinkle rest of nuts on top. Shake cinnamon on top. Bake 1
hour. Cool in pan on rack. Remove from pan and shake additional cinnamon
on top.

MRS. C. A. MATTHEWS

CRANBERRY UPSIDE DOWN CAKE

2 cups fresh cranberries	½ cup butter
½ cup sugar	¼ cup Crisco
½ cup chopped pecans	1 cup plain flour
2 eggs	Dream Whip
1 cup sugar	

Preheat oven 325°. Grease 10" pyrex pie plate. Spread clean, raw berries on
bottom of pie plate. Sprinkle ½ cup sugar and pecans over berries. Cream
eggs, sugar, butter and Crisco. Stir in flour. Pour over top of cranberry
mixture. Bake 30-45 minutes. Serve warm and top with Dream Whip.

ROSIE'S CHOCOLATE CAKE

*This cake can be made ahead as it keeps beautifully for days staying very
moist. You may wish to substitute brandy or bourbon for rum. Serve with
whipped cream or ice cream.*

1 pkg. yellow cake mix	¼ cup rum
½ cup oil	1 tsp. vanilla
1 pkg. instant chocolate pudding	1-6 oz. package chocolate chips
1-8 oz. carton sour cream	1 cup chopped pecans
4 eggs	

Mix all ingredients except the chocolate chips and pecans, and beat for 3
or 4 minutes. Add chocolate chips and pecans. Mix well. Pour into well
greased bundt pan and bake for 1 hour.

MRS. ROBERT STICKLEY

SUGAR PLUM CAKE WITH LEMON GLAZE

A simple, freezable cake with flavor coming from the unexpected strained baby food! Lemon glaze adds even more interest.

2 cups self-rising flour
2 cups granulated sugar
1 tsp. cinnamon
1 tsp. cloves
1 tsp. nutmeg
1 cup salad oil

2 small jars Gerber strained
   plums with tapioca
3 beaten eggs
1 cup chopped pecans
1 cup confectioner's sugar
juice of 2 lemons

Preheat oven to 350°. Grease well and flour tube or bundt pan. Sift together the flour, granulated sugar, cinnamon, cloves and nutmeg. Stir in the oil, plums and eggs. Add nuts. Pour into prepared pan and bake for 1 hour. Remove cake from oven and while still in pan punch holes in it with an ice pick. Over the warm cake pour a glaze made from confectioner's sugar and lemon juice. After 15 or 20 minutes turn out of pan.

MRS. F. BROCKENBROUGH LINEWEAVER

CRANBERRY NUT CAKE

2 cups flour
1 cup sugar
1½ tsp. baking powder
½ tsp. salt
¼ cup shortening

¾ cup orange juice
1 T. grated orange rind
1 egg (well beaten)
½ cup chopped nuts
1 cup chopped cranberries

Preheat oven to 350°. Sift flour, sugar, baking powder, baking soda, and salt together. Cut in shortening. Combine orange juice, rind and egg. Pour into flour mixture and stir just to dampen. Fold in nuts and cranberries. Pour batter into greased loaf pan. Bake 45 to 50 minutes or until straw comes out clean.

CHEESECAKE

A good cheesecake is compulsory fare during the holidays. This freezable beauty should more than meet your requirements.

4 large pkgs. Philadelphia
   cream cheese (softened)
5 eggs
2 cups sugar
3 T. melted butter

2 T. lemon juice
2 tsp. vanilla
3½ to 4 T. Cornstarch
1 pint sour cream

Preheat oven 325-350°. Cream together cheese and sugar. Add eggs one at a time. Add remaining ingredients and beat for 15 minutes. Put in a greased and floured spring form pan. Bake one hour. Do not open oven. Turn oven off and leave in oven an additional hour. Leave in pan overnight. Refrigerate and serve cold.

MRS. VANCE W. BRABHAM, III

CHOCOLATE CHEESECAKE

A must for all your cheesecake loving guests!

3 T. butter (melted)
1½ cups vanilla wafer crumbs
3 T. sugar
      or
substitute ground-up Oreo
   cookies for the above

3 pkg. (8 oz.) cream cheese
1 cup sugar
¼ cup cocoa
1½ tsp. vanilla
3 eggs
½ cup heavy cream

Preheat oven 350°. Combine first three ingredients and press in spring form pan. Beat cheese until smooth. Add sugar, cocoa, vanilla, and eggs one at a time. Blend in cream. Pour mixture over crumbs. Bake 50 minutes. Cool and refrigerate.

PEGGY BRAME

LIMELIGHT PIE

Great any season, but especially colorful during the holidays. A marvelous dessert for bridge. For variety you may want to substitute lemon juice for the lime.

Crust:

¼ tsp. salt
¾ cup sifted flour
2 T. sugar

¼ cup shortening
½ sq. chocolate (unsweetened)
2 T. cold water

Sift together salt, flour and sugar. Cut in shortening until size of small peas. Drip ½ square melted chocolate over mixture tossing lightly with fork. While stirring, sprinkle 1 to 2 T. cold water over mixture until moist enough to hold together. Form into a ball. Roll out on floured pastry cloth to 10″ circle. Fit loosely into 8″ pan. Fold edge to form rim. Prick with fork. Bake 400° — 10 to 12 minutes.

Filling:

15 oz. can sweetened condensed
   milk
¼ cup lime juice

¼ tsp. salt
1 cup crushed pineapple
4 drops green food coloring

Combine milk, lime juice and salt. Blend in 1 cup well drained pineapple and food coloring. Pour into cooled pie shell and chill 2-3 hours.

Topping:

¾ cup heavy cream
1 T. confectioner's sugar
½ tsp. vanilla

1 T. grated chocolate sq.
   (unsweetened)

Whip cream until stiff. Fold in sugar and vanilla. Spread over pie. Sprinkle with grated chocolate.

MRS. G. K. LEEMON, JR., ASHEVILLE, N.C.

STRAWBERRY-BANANA PIE

Another combination of fresh fruits may be substituted for the berries and bananas.

1 baked 9" pie crust
sliced berries and bananas

Orange Sauce:

½ cup sugar
⅛ tsp. salt
1 T. corn starch

½ cup orange juice
2 T. lemon juice
¼ cup plus 2 T. water

Topping:

1 pt. whipping cream
1 small can crushed pineapple, drained
¼ cup chopped pecans

In medium sized sauce pan, mix together sugar, salt and corn starch. Stir in liquid ingredients. Bring to boil and boil 1 minute or until thickened. Place sliced fruit in baked pie crust. Pour orange sauce over fruit. Allow to cool while preparing topping. Whip cream and fold in pineapple. Spread over filling and sprinkle with chopped nuts.

DANA LACY

SOUTHERN PECAN PIE

A super easy, traditional dessert. May be served with whipped cream or ice cream.

½ stick margarine (room
temperature)
½ cup sugar
3 eggs beaten

1 cup light Karo syrup
1 cup chopped nuts
1 tsp. vanilla

Preheat oven 350°. Cream margarine and sugar well. Add eggs and Karo syrup. Mix well. Add nuts and vanilla. Pour in unbaked pie shell and bake 45 minutes.

MRS. TED A. STURM

PUMPKIN PIE

1 unbaked pastry shell

Filling:

½ cup sugar
½ cup brown sugar
1¼ tsp. cinnamon
¼ tsp. cloves
¼ tsp. ginger
¼ tsp. nutmeg

1 tsp. salt
3 egg yolks (beaten)
1½ cup pumpkin
¾ cup milk
3 stiffly beaten egg whites

Preheat oven 450°. Mix sugars, spices and salt together. Add beaten egg yolks to pumpkin; then mix well with spices. Add milk. Fold in egg whites and pour into unbaked pie shell. Bake 10 minutes. Reduce to 375° and bake 30 minutes more.

MRS. JOHN W. BLACK

FROZEN STRAWBERRY PIE

A delightful light dessert with a holiday color. Put one in the freezer to have for holiday guests or a family treat after a busy day of shopping.

1 pkg. (10 oz.) frozen strawberries	½ pint whipping cream,
1 cup sugar	whipped with
2 egg whites	1 tsp. vanilla
1 T. lemon juice	1 cooked pie shell
⅛ tsp. salt	

Combine and beat first 5 ingredients with electric mixer until super thick and holds a peak. Fold in whipped cream mixture carefully. Put into a pie shell. Freeze several hours. Take out a few minutes before serving.

MRS. OTIS N. FISHER

CHOCOLATE PIE

A fabulous version of an old favorite. A real asset to any holiday entertaining.

2 heaping T. cocoa	1 tsp. vanilla
1 T. plain flour	3 egg whites
3 egg yolks	⅛ tsp. salt
1 cup sugar	⅛ tsp. cream of tartar
1 T. butter	unbaked pie shell
1 small can Pet milk	

Preheat oven to 350°. Add a small amount of hot water to cocoa to make paste. Add flour and beaten egg yolks. Beat sugar in well. Add butter then Pet milk and vanilla. Beat. Pour into unbaked pie shell and bake 30 minutes. Beat egg whites with salt and cream of tartar until stiff but not too dry. Spread on pie and close edges. Brown at 400° for 5-10 minutes.

FRENCH SILK PIE

A very rich, very elegant dessert. Best after a light meal.

Crust:

½ cup brown sugar	½ cup chopped pecans
1 cup flour	¼ lb. butter (room temperature)

Combine ingredients by stirring and place in 9 x 13 pan. Bake 10-15 minutes at 400°. Stir again and chill.

Filling:

½ lb. butter (room temp.)	3 sq. chocolate (melted)
1½ cup granulated sugar	½ tsp. peppermint extract
2 tsp. vanilla	(optional)
4 eggs	

Cream together butter and sugar. Add vanilla then eggs. Beat five minutes after each egg. Stir in chocolate and peppermint, if desired. Fill crust and chill overnight. Top with whipped cream.

MRS. KENNETH C. ROYALL

Greetings
with
Gifts

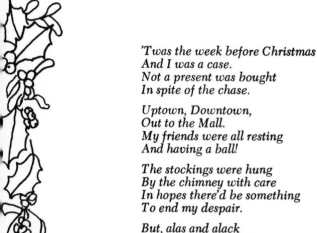

'Twas the week before Christmas
And I was a case.
Not a present was bought
In spite of the chase.

Uptown, Downtown,
Out to the Mall.
My friends were all resting
And having a ball!

The stockings were hung
By the chimney with care
In hopes there'd be something
To end my despair.

But, alas and alack
With nothing to show,
The panic within me
Was beginning to grow.

When what to my wondering
eyes did appear
But a book full of recipes.
What an idea!

I flew to the kitchen
And quick as a flash,
I created a miracle
And saved lots of cash.

My friends how they cheered
And how they did rave
At thoughts of the time
And the money I'd saved!

And I heard them exclaim
To all far and near.
We do hereby proclaim,
"Just wait till next year."

HOLIDAY PACKAGING IDEAS

Give beverage mixes in antique canning jars with glass lids which can be found at flea markets or antique shops. Attach small ribbon to wire clasp.

Powdered beverage mixes keep well when contained in crocks or cookie jars.

INSTANT RUSSIAN TEA

Here's an easy food gift idea that can be made ahead of time, keeps for months and requires no baking.

2 cups Tang	¼ cup instant dry lemonade mix
1 cup instant tea (unflavored Nestea)	1 tsp. cinnamon
	½ tsp. cloves

Mix above ingredients well and store in an air tight container. To serve use one teaspoon to a cup of hot water.

MRS. JAMES S. STRATFORD

INSTANT HOT CHOCOLATE MIX

An easy, do ahead recipe that is great to have on hand to serve guests on a cold night. Makes a super gift when cleverly packaged. Yields bunches, but if you don't want that much you can easily halve the ingredients.

Box of instant dry milk that makes into 8 quarts	1 cup confectioner's sugar
6 oz. jar Coffee-mate	1 lb. can Nestle's hot chocolate

Mix all ingredients together in large (like a roaster) sized container. Store in large tupperware container until ready to measure out for gifts or for drinks. To serve: mix ¼ to ⅓ cup of mix with hot water.

MRS. KENT DAVIDSON

HOLIDAY PACKAGING IDEAS

Package a loaf of bread for giving by tying a bright bandana around the loaf.

For holiday giving put bread or small loaf cakes in a basket and tie with colorful ribbon. If you choose a bread basket you may wish to wrap the contents with a colorful napkin or piece of fabric cut to napkin size.

For a unique gift place bread or loaf cake on a wooden or lucite cutting board and wrap board and bread in clear wrap. Attach a huge bow at the handle of the board. You may find your friendly glass cutter will cut lucite boards for you from your design.

Put bread sticks or sesame sticks in a large size pencil holder, acquired at the dime store then covered by you with lovely sea shells. A mug or pitcher would also be perfect to contain this food gift.

A cake placed on a pretty tray and covered in clear wrap makes a nice gift after the cake is long gone.

Home-baked items will stay freshest in your freezer. Wrap bread or rolls in heavy plastic bags or freezer-strength foil. Large coffee cake may be supported with cardboard, then sealed in freezer foil before being stored in the freezer. To serve frozen coffee cake, heat in wrapping, in 350° oven for 15-20 minutes or until cake has been thoroughly thawed and is heated through. Stir a little cream or fruit juice into confectioner's sugar — then add a fresh glaze when cake comes from the oven.

ORANGE FRUIT CUPCAKES

Especially good for a holiday breakfast or brunch, these cupcakes are so moist and tasty. They improve with age, and are freezable.

½ cup margarine (room temp.)	2 cups all purpose flour
1 cup sugar	½ tsp. soda
2 eggs	½ cup chopped nuts
¾ cup buttermilk (room temp.)	1 cup chopped dates

Preheat oven 350°. Grease miniature muffin pans with Crisco. Cream together butter and sugar. Add eggs one at a time and buttermilk alternately. Add flour that has been sifted with soda. Mix well with mixer. Place chopped nuts in bowl. Chop dates in same bowl so they will not stick together. Add dates and nuts to other ingredients. Place in prepared pans and bake for 15 minutes.

Topping:

1½ cups sugar
¾ cups real orange juice, not frozen

Put topping in double boiler. Let sugar dissolve and keep warm. Allow cupcakes to cool 5 minutes before dipping in topping. Completely submerge cupcakes in topping while still warm and place on waxed paper to cool. Store in air tight container or freeze.

MRS. VAN WOLTZ

BANANA NUT BREAD

So easy to fix, economical, and freezable, but does dirty three bowls.

1 cup sugar
1 stick oleo
2 cups flour
1 tsp. soda
⅛ tsp. salt

2 whole eggs, beaten
1 tsp. vanilla
2 ripe bananas
½ cup chopped pecans (2 oz. pkg.)

Preheat oven to 350°. Grease loaf pan. Cream sugar and oleo in large mixing bowl. In another bowl sift together flour, soda, and salt. Add sifted ingredients to sugar and oleo. Add beaten eggs and vanilla. Mash bananas with fork until mushy. Add mashed bananas and chopped pecans to other ingredients. Pour into pans and bake approximately 1 hour.

MRS. DANIEL W. FOUTS

HERB BREAD

2 pkg. dry yeast
2 cups milk, scalded and cooled
   slightly
1 cup chicken stock
1 T. sugar

1 T. salt
1 scant cup shortening
4 cups white flour
2 cups whole wheat flour
3 tsp. mixed herbs (thyme,
   rosemary, parsley, tarragon)

Preheat oven to 300°. Grease 2 standard-sized loaf pans. In large mixing bowl dissolve yeast in warm milk. Add chicken stock, sugar, salt, shortening, herbs, all of the whole wheat flour, and 2 cups of the white flour. Mix well. Knead in the remaining two cups of white flour until dough is smooth and elastic. Cover and let rise until double. Push down, knead, and divide into 2 parts. Put in prepared pans and let rise until double. Bake 1 hour.

MRS. CHARLES W. CLONINGER, JR.

PEAR BREAD

An easy, freezable bread, moist and tasty. To add a decorative touch sprinkle with powdered sugar.

½ cup softened oleo
½ cup brown sugar, firmly packed
½ cup sugar
1 egg
2 cups flour
1 tsp. baking soda

½ tsp. allspice
1 tsp. cinnamon
½ tsp. salt
2 cups chopped canned pears
   (no juice)
⅔ cups chopped pecans

Preheat oven to 350°. Grease loaf pan. Cream oleo and sugars. Add egg. Beat well. Sift together flour, soda, allspice, cinnamon, and salt. Add to shortening mixture, then stir in pears and nuts. Pour into prepared pan and bake for 1 hour. Let stand and cool.

MRS. JOHN M. WOLTZ, JR.

WHOLE WHEAT PECAN BREAD

You need this bread around as it is so simple and does not require kneading. Makes a great gift and can be kept frozen indefinitely. For added variety substitute wheat germ for all or half of the pecans.

2¼ cups unsifted white flour	1 cup milk
1 cup sifted whole wheat flour	¼ cup water
2 T. firmly packed light brown sugar	1 T. margarine
1 tsp. salt	¾ cup toasted chopped pecans (chop in blender)
1 pkg. active dry yeast	

Preheat oven to 375°. Grease 8½"x4½"x2½" loaf pan or two small loaf pans. Combine flours. In a large bowl thoroughly mix 1 cup flour mixture, brown sugar, salt, and undissolved dry yeast. Combine milk, water, and margarine in a sauce pan. Heat over low heat until liquids are very warm (120°-130°). Margarine does not need to melt. Gradually add to dry ingredients and beat two minutes at medium speed. Add ½ cup flour mixture or enough flour mixture to make a thick batter. Beat at high speed 2 minutes. Add pecans. Stir in enough additional flour mixture to make a soft dough (may need to add additional white flour). Cover, let rise in warm place, free from draft, until doubled in bulk, about 40 minutes. Punch dough down; turn out onto heavily floured board. Shape into loaf. Place in pan. Cover; let rise until doubled in bulk. Bake about 35 minutes. Remove from pan.

SOUR CREAM COFFEE CAKE

What a welcome gift for anyone on your Christmas list; a great coffee cake for Christmas morning that they don't have to do a thing to but eat!

½ lb. margarine	2 cups flour
1 cup sugar	1 tsp. soda
2 eggs	½ tsp. salt
1 tsp. vanilla	1 tsp. baking powder
1 cup sour cream	

Preheat oven to 350°. Grease and flour 2-8 or 9 inch pie pans. Cream margarine and sugar. Add eggs and vanilla. Sift dry ingredients and add alternately with sour cream to mixture of margarine and sugar. Place ½ of mixture in each pan.

The Topping:

½ cup sugar	1 T. cinnamon
½ cup chopped nuts	

Mix the above together. Sprinkle ½ of topping on each pie. Cut topping into mixture with a knife and then bake for 25 minutes.

MRS. NOLLIE W. NEILL

PUMPKIN BREAD

An old favorite for the holidays, but this recipe has a surprise ingredient; an orange. Can be frozen indefinitely.

⅔ cup Crisco
2⅔ cup sugar
4 eggs
1 lb. can pumpkin
⅓ cup water
3⅓ cup regular flour
½ tsp. baking powder
2 tsp. soda

1½ tsp. salt
1 tsp. cinnamon
1 tsp. ground cloves
⅔ cup raisins
1 whole orange (cut into
   quarters, seeds removed)
⅔ cup chopped pecans

Preheat oven to 350°. Grease and flour 2 standard-sized loaf pans or 4 small loaf pans. Cream together in large mixing bowl shortening and sugar. Add eggs, pumpkin, and water. Sift together: flour, baking powder, baking soda, salt, cinnamon, and cloves. Add flour mixture to pumpkin mixture. Use blender to chop: raisins, orange, and half of ⅓ cup of water. Then add ⅔ cup nuts and rest of the water, mixing well. Add raisin mixture to above mixture. Mix thoroughly and pour into prepared pans. Bake 1 hour.

MRS. ROBERT P. FOXWORTH

BANANA BREAD

Always a favorite, this do ahead banana bread can be frozen for later delivery or served warm for a holiday breakfast.

1 cup sugar
1½ tsp. soda
1½ cups flour
½ tsp. salt
1 egg

½ cup salad oil
1 tsp. vanilla
3 T. milk
3 very ripe mashed bananas
½ cup chopped nuts

Preheat oven to 350°. Grease and flour 2 medium-sized or 4 small loaf pans. Sift dry ingredients together in large bowl. Beat eggs, and mix with salad oil, vanilla and milk. Add egg mixture to dry ingredients. Mix well and then add mashed bananas and nuts. Pour into pans and bake for 40 minutes.

MRS. C. ALLAN MATTHEWS

SPOON BREAD

Surprise a neighbor over the holidays with some hot spoon bread.

1 cup corn meal
4 cups milk
2 T. butter

1¾ tsp. salt
4 eggs well beaten

Preheat oven to 400°. Grease a 1½ qt. baking dish. Cook corn meal and milk until it is the consistency of thin mush (about 5 minutes). Add salt and butter. Fold well-beaten eggs slowly into mixture. Pour into baking dish and bake 45 minutes.

MRS. MACK R. LEATH

HOLIDAY PACKAGING IDEAS

Fruitcake: Keeps very well in a plastic or metal container with a close-fitting lid. You may wish to wrap fruitcake in a cloth dipped in a little sweet wine or brandy to prevent it from drying out.

MINIATURE FRUIT CUPCAKES

A rich, delicious and beautiful Christmas food gift idea. For variety substitute bourbon for grapefruit juice.

¼ lb. real butter
1 cup brown sugar (firmly
   packed)
2 eggs
2½ cups flour
½ tsp. salt
1 T. milk

¾ cup grapefruit juice
1 lb. pecan pieces
¾ cup candied pineapple pieces
¾ cup candied red cherries
¾ cup candied green cherries
2 cups mixed fruit pieces or
   date pieces

Preheat oven to 350°. Mix butter and sugar. Then add one egg at a time. Mix remaining ingredients except grapefruit juice and spoon into mini-muffin tins lined with paper cups. Bake for 20-25 minutes. Sprinkle several drops of grapefruit juice over each after baking and store in tins. Makes 72 cupcakes.

MRS. JAMES B. STRATFORD

WHITE FRUIT CAKE

A Christmas favorite that is made weeks in advance, and will remain fresh throughout the Holidays if stored in an airtight cake tin with apple wedges.

½ lb. margarine
1 cup sugar
2 cups plain flour
5 or 6 eggs, beaten
½ tsp. baking powder

1 lb. candied cherries
   red, green, yellow
1 lb. candied pineapple
4 cups pecans
2 T. vanilla
1 T. lemon extract

Line tube cake pan with brown paper. Have paper to extend 1″ higher than pan. Be sure to line bottom and tube part too. Sift flour, and then measure it. Add baking powder. Cream together flour mixture and margarine. In separate large bowl mix beaten eggs with the sugar, vanilla and lemon extract. Add flour mixture and mix thoroughly. Then add fruits and nuts (fruit should be sliced and the nuts broken up). When all ingredients are well mixed, place evenly in pan and bake for 2½ hours at 275°. Let cake cool completely before removing from pan. Then peel brown paper off, and store in airtight cake tin with apple wedges added.

MRS. ROBERT BAYNES

CARROT CAKE

This perennial favorite is so simple to make and tastes great. Best when served cold. Don't give away the secret and young guests will never know they're eating common garden variety carrots.

2 cups sugar	2 cups plain flour
1 cup Wesson oil	2 tsp. baking soda
4 eggs	2 tsp. cinnamon
3 cups grated carrots (5 or 6)	1 tsp. salt

Preheat oven to 325°. Have ready 3 round-layer cake pans. Cream sugar, oil and eggs. Add carrots. Sift together flour, baking soda, cinnamon and salt. Add to other ingredients, mix well, and pour into cake pans. Bake for 45 minutes.

Icing:

1-8 oz. pkg. cream cheese (room temperature)	1 tsp. vanilla
	1 box confectioner's sugar
1 stick butter (room temperature)	1 cup chopped walnuts

Mix together cream cheese, butter, vanilla and confectioner's sugar. Ice each layer and sprinkle with nuts.

MRS. JOSEPH E. JOHNSON

LEMON JELLO POUND CAKE

A simple to make and simply delicious freezable cake. Be sure to put tin foil under and around sides of cake to prevent glaze from running off.

1 pgk. Duncan Hines yellow cake mix	4 eggs
	⅔ cups salad oil
1 small pkg. lemon Jello	⅔ cup water

Preheat oven to 325°. Grease and flour a Bundt cake pan. Put all ingredients in a large bowl and beat 3 minutes with a mixer. Bake 55-60 minutes. Turn out cake while still warm and pour orange glaze over top.

Orange glaze:

¼ cup butter or margarine	⅓ cup orange juice (not frozen)
⅔ cup sugar	1 T. grated orange rind

Heat glaze ingredients in a saucepan until sugar has dissolved.

MRS. SHANKS WILBORN, SOUTH BOSTON, VA.

BISHOP'S CAKE

3 eggs	1 cup candied cherries (chopped)
1 cup sugar	1 cup chopped dates
1½ cups flour	1 pkg. (12 oz.) semi-sweet
1½ tsp. baking powder	chocolate chips
¼ tsp. salt	2 cups chopped walnuts

Preheat oven to 325°. Line loaf pan with waxed paper. Combine eggs and sugar. Beat well. Sift dry ingredients. Add coarsely chopped fruit, chocolate and nuts to dry ingredients. Add to egg mixture. Bake 1½ hours in prepared pan. Store in closed container.

CAROL vonCANNON

RUM CAKE WITH GLAZE

A fantastic phony, this cake tastes like it's made with the real thing . . . while white wine is the key. So easy to put together and an elegant treat for guests or gifts. Good for days after baking . . . but so good it'll be gone in a jiffy!

½ cup chopped pecans (2 oz. pkg.)
1 pkg. Duncan Hines butter cake mix
1 small box instant vanilla pudding
½ cup white wine
½ cup water
½ cup cooking oil
4 eggs

Preheat oven to 350°. Grease and flour 10" tube pan. Sprinkle chopped pecans in bottom of pan. Combine all other ingredients and mix for 2 minutes. Bake 50-60 minutes.

Glaze:

1 cup sugar
1 stick butter
½ cup white wine
½ cup water

Mix glaze ingredients in saucepan and boil for 2-3 minutes. Drizzle over cake.

MRS. KENNETH C. ROYALL, III

FRESH APPLE GINGERBREAD

Try this do ahead, freezable gingerbread recipe with a flavor twist. Especially good served warm and topped with whipped cream. Try it also with warm applesauce on top.

½ cup butter or margarine
½ cup sugar
2 eggs
⅔ cup molasses
1½ tsp. baking soda
¾ tsp. cream of tartar
¾ tsp. salt
½ tsp. nutmeg
¼ tsp. cloves
1 tsp. ground ginger
½ tsp. cinnamon
1¼ cup grated apple, including peeling, (quarter and core first to make it easier)
⅓ cup milk
2 cups flour (sift before measuring)

(Optional: 1 cup raisins or chopped dates, or ¾ cup nuts).

Preheat oven to 350°. Grease and flour standard loaf pan. Cream together first three ingredients. Add molasses. Beat at high speed for 1 minute. Add next 7 ingredients; mix well. Fold in apples and milk, then add flour, one cup at a time. Add any optional ingredients last. Pour into prepared pan and bake for one hour or until cake tests done (clean toothpick or cake tester). Cool in pan for 10 minutes; turn onto rack.

MRS. KENT DAVIDSON

MINI PECAN TARTS

These marvelous tarts can be oven ready in just 30 minutes. The dough can be made in 10 minutes and refrigerated until ready for use.

1-3 oz. pkg. cream cheese
  (room temperature)
½ cup margarine or butter
  (room temperature)
1 cup flour
1 egg

¾ cup brown sugar
1 T. soft margarine or butter
1 tsp. vanilla
dash salt
¾ cup pecans

Preheat oven to 325°. Soften cream cheese and margarine to room temperature, then blend with flour. Chill this mixture 1 hour. Shape into 1" balls and press into ungreased mini-muffin pans. Beat until smooth the egg, brown sugar, 1 T. margarine, vanilla, and salt. Divide pecans in half. Spoon half the chopped pecans onto the bottom of tarts. Spoon filling over pecans. Top with remaining pecans. Bake 25 minutes. Cool and remove from pans by gently loosening edge with knife point. Makes 24 tarts.

DOROTHY SOUCHON, SAN ANTONIO, TEXAS

FRENCH MINT TARTS

A unique, cupcake sized dessert gift for the holiday hostess. Can be made ahead, frozen, then thawed 10 minutes before serving.

3 egg whites
1 cup sugar
15 saltine cracker squares

1 cup chopped nuts
1 tsp. vanilla

Preheat oven to 350°. Beat whites until stiff. Add sugar, crushed saltine crackers and nuts. Mix well. Add vanilla. Put 1 tsp. mixture in cupcake containers placed in muffin tins. Bake 20 minutes and cool.

Topping:

1 cup softened butter
2 cups confectioner's sugar
4 squares melted chocolate

4 eggs
1 tsp. mint
2 tsp. vanilla

Beat butter and sugar for 5 minutes. Blend in melted chocolate. Add eggs one at a time and beat well. Add flavorings. Put mixture on top of cup cakes and freeze.

MRS. JAMES D. HUCKABEE, III

DAMSON PIE

A easy pie recipe that can be done when you have time and frozen until needed. Especially good when served warm and à la mode.

1 cup Damson preserves
½ cup sugar
½ cup melted butter
1 T. flour

2 eggs
1 tsp. vanilla
½ cup milk
1 unbaked pastry shell

Mix the ingredients in the order given. Bake at 350° for 10 minutes. Then bake at 275° for 15 minutes longer. Serve warm.

HOLIDAY PACKAGING IDEAS

Any canister will hold lots of cookies. You may wish to decorate the outside with polka dot ribbon or ball fringe for a colorful gift.

Cookies wrapped in clear wrap and placed in a wire colander promise a gift that will be appreciated for years to come.

Place cookies on a new cookie sheet and wrap in clear wrap for giving to one of your favorite cooks.

A fish bowl filled with cookies, minus the fish of course, would delight an adult or child.

Clay or lucite flower pots hold cookies wrapped in clear wrap very well. For a special touch you may wish to cover the pots with squares of material for a patchwork effect or paint them with acrylic paints in a unique design. Guaranteed to thrill the plant buff.

For children or your children's friends place cookies in toy wagons, cowboy hats, doll cradle, lunch pail, or sand bucket.

Cookies: Store soft and crisp cookies separately. Soft cookies need to be tightly covered; crisp cookies will stay crisp longer if the container has a loose-fitting lid. If your cookie jar is full to overflowing, wrap extra cookies and freeze. Nearly all cookies freeze well.

CHRISTMAS FRUIT COOKIE

An easy, freezable cookie that stays moist (like fruit cake) for months. Recipe yields 8 dozen.

½ lb. each of the following:
   cut cherries
   cut citron
   cut pineapple
1 lb. white raisins
1 cup sherry
3 eggs
1½ cups light brown sugar
3 cups flour

⅔ cup butter (melted)
1 tsp. soda
1 T. buttermilk
1 tsp. cloves
2 tsp. cinnamon
1 tsp. vanilla
½ lb. almonds, cut or slivered
½ lb. pecans

Soak the cut fruit overnight in one cup sherry. Preheat oven to 300-350°. Grease cookie sheets. Mix batter and add fruit, then nuts. Drop by teaspoons on prepared sheet. Bake 10-12 minutes.

MRS. ROBERT H. CALDWELL

LACE COOKIES

Here's a quick cookie that is delicious and keeps for weeks when stored in an airtight container.

½ cup margarine
½ cup light corn syrup
½ cup firmly packed brown sugar

1 cup all purpose flour (sifted)
1 cup pecans (finely chopped)
1 tsp. vanilla

Preheat oven to 350°. Cover with foil and grease cookie sheets. Combine margarine, corn syrup, and brown sugar in heavy, medium sized saucepan. Heat just to boiling over medium heat, stirring constantly. Remove from heat. Stir in flour, pecans, and vanilla. Drop by scant teaspoonfuls, 3" apart on prepared cookie sheets. Bake 8 minutes or until light golden brown. Let cookies remain on sheets a few seconds to stiffen a bit. Immediately, place on paper toweling to cool. When cool store in air tight container.

MRS. ROBERT H. CALDWELL

LACE COOKIE VARIATION

Substitute 1 cup chopped, flaked coconut for pecans. Combine coconut with flour before adding to sugar mixture.

MRS. SEWALL H. DIXON, JR.

NANNIE'S COOKIES

A melt-in-your-mouth, remember-when-you-were-a-kid-cookie! Great anytime, but especially nice to share this old favorite with friends at Christmas.

1 stick butter
2 cups brown sugar
2 eggs (beaten)
1 tsp. vanilla

1 heaping cup of plain flour
1 tsp. baking powder
1 cup chopped nuts

Preheat oven to 325°. Cream butter and sugar. Add eggs and vanilla. Add flour, baking powder and nuts. Drop by teaspoonfuls on ungreased cookie sheet. Bake 20-25 minutes.

MRS. RAY L. COX

ANGEL WHISPERS

Don't let the length of instructions scare you. This super easy recipe really takes very little time and makes a unique, attractive and tasty cookie.

1st Day:
The Dough:

1 cup butter
½ cup powdered sugar (sifted)
1 tsp. lemon extract

2 cups flour (sifted)
¼ tsp. salt

Cream butter and sugar. Add remaining ingredients, blend well and chill overnight.

The filling:

3 T. lemon juice
²⁄₃ cup sugar
1 egg (slightly beaten)

1½ T. softened butter
Grated lemon peel

Combine lemon juice and sugar in double boiler. Gradually add egg. Add butter and lemon peel. Stir constantly and cook until thickened. Chill overnight.

2nd Day:

Take dough out and let it sit at room temperature an hour or so. Take a level teaspoonful, roll into a ball and flatten slightly on greased cookie sheet. Bake at 375° for 8 minutes, until edges are just brown. Cool and spread a small amount of filling between two cookies. Refrigerate covered until ready to serve.

MRS. THOMAS P. HOWELL, LOOKOUT MOUNTAIN, TENN.

POUND CAKE COOKIES

These small in size but big in taste cookies will be a welcome treat for any one on your Christmas list. So easy to make, they can be done at the last minute.

2½ sticks butter
1 cup sugar
2 egg yolks

2¾ cups flour
1 tsp. vanilla

Preheat oven to 350°. Grease cookie sheets. Mix the above ingredients together and drop one inch apart by teaspoonfuls on cookie sheet. Bake 10-12 minutes. Let stand until warm, then place in refrigerator.

MRS. JAMES S. STRATFORD

MINCE MEAT COOKIES

A new use for mincemeat, especially good at holiday time.

1 cup softened butter
1½ cups sugar
3 eggs (beaten well)
1 tsp. soda
1½ tsp. hot water

½ tsp. salt
3¼ cups flour
1 cup chopped walnuts
1 cup mincemeat

Preheat oven to 350°. Grease cookie sheets. Cream butter. Add sugar gradually. Add eggs and then soda dissolved in water. Mix and sift salt and ½ of the flour. Add to above. Next add nuts, mincemeat and the remainder of the flour. Mix well. Drop by spoonfuls on prepared sheets and bake until done.

MRS. J. M. DOWTIN, JR.

CATHEDRAL WINDOW COOKIES

A quick and easy way to make a fudge that is a favorite with the children.
For variety substitute white mini-marshmallows for the colored ones. Pre-
pare at least a day before serving.

1 stick margarine
1-12 oz. pkg. chocolate bits
1 cup chopped nuts

1 large pkg. colored, miniature
marshmallows

Melt margarine and chocolate bits. Allow to cool, then add marshmallows.
Add nuts and mix well. Shape into two logs on waxed paper. Roll up in
waxed paper and store overnight in refrigerator. Slice to desired thickness
with sharp or electric knife. Cut each slice into quarters and keep stored in
tin in refrigerator. Yields 4 dozen.

MRS. ROBERT HOOD CALDWELL

KRIS KRINGLES

½ cup butter
¼ cup sugar
1 beaten egg yolk (reserve
egg white in separate bowl)
1 T. grated orange peel

1 tsp. lemon juice
1 cup plain flour
dash salt
½ cup nuts (crushed)
9 candied cherries (red or green)

Preheat oven to 325°. Cream butter and sugar. Add egg yolk, lemon and
orange peels, and lemon juice. Beat thoroughly. Stir in flour and salt. Chill
until firm. Form into small balls. Dip in slightly beaten egg white and roll
in crushed nuts. Press a half cherry in center. Bake 20 minutes.

MRS. RALPH J. GOLDEN

DATE WALNUT DELIGHT

These "Christmasy" favorites, date and nut cookies, are easy to make, freeze
well, and can be stored in tins for a good while.

½ cup margarine (room temp.)
¾ cup sugar
2 egg yolks
1 tsp. vanilla
1¼ cup sifted plain flour
½ tsp. soda
Dash of salt
1-8 oz. pkg. diced Bordo dates or whole Bordo dates (cut up)

½ tsp. cinnamon
⅛ tsp. ground cloves
1 T. sour milk (add a few drops
vinegar to whole milk)
½ lb. (2 cups) chopped black
walnuts

Preheat oven to 325°. Grease cookie sheets well. Cream butter and sugar
thoroughly. Add egg yolks and vanilla. Beat well. Sift together flour, soda,
salt and spices. Add alternately along with sour milk to egg mixture blending in well. Mix in walnuts and dates. Drop with tsp. onto prepared cookie
sheets. Bake 20 minutes.

MRS. LUCY SMITH

FRUIT NUT CHRISTMAS WREATHS

These cookies are as "Dressy" as they are delicious.

1 cup soft butter
½ cup packed brown sugar
1 egg
2 cups flour
½ tsp. baking powder

1 cup quick oatmeal
½ cup chopped pecans
¼ cup finely chopped candied
   cherries
½ cup shredded coconut

Preheat oven to 350°. Beat butter till creamy. Add sugar. Beat until fluffy. Beat in egg. Sift flour and baking powder together and add to butter mixture. Stir in oatmeal, nuts, and cherries. With greased hands, shape into doughnut type wreaths. Place on ungreased cookie sheet about 2″ apart. Bake for 12-15 minutes. When cool, frost with green glaze. Sprinkle with coconut and decorate with additional tiny pieces of candied cherries.

Green sugar glaze:
   ¾ cup powdered sugar
   3 to 4 tsp. water
   Tint with green food coloring
   Yields 3½ dozen.

MRS. JACK UPTON

LEMON MERINGUE SQUARES

Great to have on hand for holiday entertaining. Can be made ahead and refrigerated until ready to use.

2 cups flour
½ cup powdered sugar
½ tsp. salt

1½ sticks softened butter
   (not whipped)

Preheat oven to 325°. Grease a 9″ x 13″ pan. Combine all ingredients and press in bottom of pan. Bake for 20 minutes. Cool slightly.

4 eggs
4 T. flour

2 cups sugar
juice of 2 lemons (⅓ cup)

Preheat oven to 350°. Beat eggs slightly and add combined flour/sugar and finally lemon juice. Pour this mixture over baked crust. Bake for 25 minutes. Remove from oven and sprinkle with confectioner's sugar. Cool and cut. Refrigerate.

BARBARA RENTENBACH

OATMEAL APRICOT BARS

An easy, freezable bar cookie with a different twist.

1½ cups sifted flour
1 tsp. baking powder
¼ tsp. salt
1½ cups quick cooking rolled oats

1 cup brown sugar
¾ cup butter or margarine
1 cup apricot jam or preserves

Preheat oven to 375°. Use 8 x 8 x 2 square pan. Sift together flour, baking powder, and salt. Stir in oats and sugar. Cut in butter until mixture is crumbly. Pat ⅔ of this mixture into pan. Spread with apricot preserves. Cover with remaining ⅓ of crumb mixture. Bake for 35 minutes or until browned. Cool. Cut in bars or squares. Yields 16 or more if small pieces.

DATE FINGERS

An unusual cookie, easy to make, and a sure favorite with family and friends. Yields 4 dozen cookies.

1 stick butter
1 cup sugar
1 egg (well beaten)
1 cup dates (chopped)

1 tsp. vanilla
2½ cups Rice Krispies
1 cup fine coconut

In medium sized saucepan, melt butter. Add sugar, beaten egg, dates and nuts. Bring slowly to boiling point, turn unit to low heat and allow to cook for 10 minutes. Stir constantly to prevent sticking. Remove from heat and add vanilla and Rice Krispies. Cook and shape in small portions about the size of little fingers. Roll in coconut.

MRS. ROBERT H. CALDWELL

WALNUT BRANDY BALLS

½ cup butter or margarine
   (room temperature)
½ cup sifted confectioners sugar
⅛ tsp. salt

1 T. brandy
½ tsp. vanilla
1 cup sifted all-purpose flour
½ cup finely chopped walnuts

Preheat oven to 325°. Cream together butter, sugar, and salt until fluffy. Stir in brandy and vanilla. Stir in flour and nuts. Mix well and shape into ¾" balls. Bake on ungreased cookie sheet for 20 minutes or until lightly brown. Roll in confectioner's sugar.

MRS. CHARLES R. BENNETT

CREME DE MENTHE BALLS

Particularly festive cookie when made with green de menthe. May be made at the last minute or done in advance and frozen until ready to use. Yields 4 dozen.

1 cup vanilla wafer crumbs
¾ cup finely chopped pecans
1 cup confectioner's sugar

2 T. light corn syrup
⅓ cup green creme de menthe
powdered sugar for coating

Mix wafers, pecans, and 1 cup sugar in medium sized bowl. Add syrup and creme de menthe. Blend well to make stiff dough. Roll into small balls. (May freeze here if desired). Once thawed, roll in powdered sugar.

MRS. JAMES E. COLLINS

HOLIDAY PACKAGING IDEAS

A large sea shell filled with nuts or mints and covered with clear wrap makes a beautiful gift.

Fill a wooden or bright plastic sugar scoop full of nuts or candy and cover in clear wrap. Tie with a huge bright bow.

Use small baskets to put nuts or mints in and place bow on handle.

Little tin buckets and watering cans make delightful containers for small items such as rum balls.

A couple of egg cups look adorable filled with candy.

A recipe box (lucite would be nice) filled with candy, nuts, or walnut brandy balls would be a lovely gift for a friend who loves to cook. You may want to include your recipe.

Parfait glasses make ideal containers for rum balls, nuts, or sesame sticks.

Nuts are good freezer candidates. Salted nuts will keep 6 months, unsalted from nine to 12 months.

Homemade soft candies don't freeze well — just pass the dish around and enjoy them while they're fresh.

PECAN BUTTER CRUNCH

A delicious and unique candy treat. One word of caution — do not make on damp or rainy days. Almonds may be substituted for pecans.

1 cup butter	3 T. water
1⅓ cups sugar	1 cup finely chopped pecans
1 T. light corn syrup	
2-6 oz. or 8 or. chocolate bars (Nestles or Hershey)	

Lightly butter 13 x 9 x 2 pan. Melt butter in large sauce pan. Add sugar, corn syrup, and water. Cook, stirring, to hard crack stage (330 degrees). Watch carefully after temperature reaches 280 degrees. Pour into prepared pan. Cool thoroughly (this takes at least two to three hours). Melt one candy bar in double boiler and spread over cooled candy. Sprinkle ½ cup nuts on chocolate. Let this dry several hours or overnight. Invert pan on waxed paper. Melt second candy bar and spread on inverted candy mixture. Sprinkle ½ cup nuts on chocolate. Let dry overnight. Break into pieces and store in closed container.

SPICED NUTS

1 cup powdered sugar	½ tsp. salt
½ tsp. cinnamon	2½ T. salad oil
¼ tsp. nutmeg	2 cups nuts

Sift together sugar, cinnamon, nutmeg and salt. Heat salad oil in skillet. Add ½ of above mixture and heat over *low* temperature, stirring constantly until sugar is dissolved and thickened. Add nuts and mix until they are coated with the syrup. Pour this on other half of sugar mixture and mix until nuts are completely covered. Allow to cool and they are ready to serve or store.

MRS. G. K. LEEMON, JR., ASHEVILLE, N. C.

ROASTED PECANS

A delightful way to remember someone at holiday time and a breeze to make at the last minute.

pecan halves   **butter**   **salt**

Preheat oven to 325°. Place pecan halves on a cookie sheet in one layer. Dot generously with butter. Bake about 10 minutes or until pecans are a little darker. Be careful not to burn! Remove from oven and salt to taste.

MRS. RICHARD W. WILLIS

MEXICAN PECAN CANDY (PRALENE)

Stuckey's, take a back seat! This super simple pralene has got you beat. Yields 4 dozen.

4 cups pecans (coarsley chopped)   **1 cup milk**
4 cups brown sugar (dark)   **3 T. butter**

Cook sugar, milk, and butter to soft ball stage on candy thermometer. Beat until it begans to thicken and is creamy. Add nuts. Drop by teaspoon on a greased baking sheet or waxed paper.

MRS. ALISE DUL, SAN ANTONIO, TEXAS

TERRIFIC FUDGE

Everybody's favorite, this simple fudge practically sets before it gets in the refrigerator.

1 large can evaporated milk   **2 sticks margarine**
2 lbs. sugar   **3 T. vanilla**
3 small pkgs. semi-sweet   **1 cup chopped nuts (optional)**
   chocolate bits

Combine milk and sugar in heavy pot. Boil exactly six minutes. Remove from heat. Add 3 pkgs. semi-sweet chocolate bits, margarine, vanilla, and nuts, stirring to blend. Pour into buttered pans and refrigerate.

MRS. PATRICK G. LANDRY, JR.

HOLIDAY PACKAGING IDEAS

Place hors d'eouvres in ice bucket to delight your favorite host and hostess.

Hors d'eouvres given in a unique wooden bowl or straw basket that can later be used for chips or crackers would be greatly appreciated by your favorite host and hostess.

CHEESE PUFFS

These easy hors d'oeuvres can be made in minutes and frozen ready for baking. Delicious when served hot.

1 loaf white (unsliced) bread, several days old	½ lb. soft sharp cheddar cheese (cubed)
6 oz. softened cream cheese	4 egg whites (beaten stiff)
1 cup butter or margarine	

Oil cookie sheets. Trim bread crusts and cut bread into 1 inch cubes. Melt together over medium heat, cream cheese, butter and cheddar cheese until of rarebit consistency (well mixed and melted). Stir constantly. Remove mixture from heat and fold in egg whites. Dip bread cubes in this warm mixture until well coated. Place on prepared cookie sheets and freeze in bags or containers. Do not defrost before baking! Bake 12-15 minutes at 400°.

MRS. ROBERT H. CALDWELL

CHEESE WAFERS

An easy do ahead hors d'oeuvres that will keep throughout the holidays in an airtight container. Can be frozen after baking and kept indefinitely.

1 stick butter or margarine (room temperature)	1 cup flour
	¼ tsp. cayenne
2 cups grated sharp cheese (room temperature)	1 cup Rice Krispies

Preheat oven to 375°. Mix all ingredients well. Roll into small balls (walnut size). Bake on cookie sheet until edges brown *slightly*. About ten minutes. Yield 4 dozen.

OLIVE JORDAN

HAM AND CHEESE BISCUITS

These delicious biscuits are so easy and can be cooked ahead, frozen and reheated in foil when ready to serve.

1 pkg. pie crust mix	1 small jar Smithfield ham spread
1 glass Old English cheese	1 small can deviled ham

Preheat oven to 450°. Blend cheese into pie crust mix adding *no water*. Mix well. Roll into large ball. Refrigerate awhile. Roll between floured waxed paper. Cut into circles with cheese jar. Mix meats together. Spread meat mixture on one side. Fold over like pocket book rolls. Seal edges. Bake for 15 minutes. Yields 40 bite sized biscuits.

MRS. THOMAS R. BEARD

HAL-PENNY CHEESE SNACK

Great on any party table, these cheesy snacks can be kept well when stored —in air tight containers. For variety press sliced green or black olives, or cooked chicken livers in slices. Bake and serve hot.

2 sticks margarine (room temp.)	2 cups flour
1 lb. grated cheddar cheese	6-8 Jalopeno peppers (hot),
1 pkg. dry onion soup mix	chopped fine
1 tsp. salt	

Preheat oven to 350°. Blend all ingredients. Roll in a 2" diameter log. Wrap in waxed paper and chill overnight or several days. Slice thinly. Bake on ungreased cookie sheet 10-12 minutes or until brown.

ALISE DUL, SAN ANTONIO, TEXAS

SESAME SEED STICKS

A quick and easy do ahead for holiday nibblers. Stays fresh for 2-3 weeks in tight container.

thin sliced Pepperidge Farms bread	2 T. dry parsley
½ lb. creamed chiffon margarine	1 tsp. tarragon leaves
2 T. sesame seeds (toasted)	1 tsp. sweet marjoram
	1 T. chives, freeze dried

Preheat oven to 300°. Decrust and cut bread slices into thirds. Spread with margarine and herb mixture. Bake on cookie sheet for 25 minutes. Store in tight container.

MRS. EDGAR B. FISHER, JR.

HOLIDAY PACKAGING IDEAS

Spreads placed in small lucite flower pots and covered with clear wrap make a delightful gift. Tie ribbon around the rim of pot. If pot has hole in bottom be sure to stop it up.

Crockery bowls or coffee mugs, are great containers for spreads, chutney, or preserves and jellies. If necessary, simply seal top with paraffin or cover with clear wrap.

Put syrups in old fashioned bottles which are the rage at flea markets everywhere. Tie bow around the neck with serving suggestions printed on a card and attached to the bow.

This snowball top can be adapted to any size jelly jar.

Materials needed:

glue   2½″ chenile stems
foam balls (1 size of lid; 5 small)   artificial holly with red berries

With glue fasten half of the larger foam ball to lid. Stick 1 chenile stem into each of the five small balls and stick to top of foam lid. Stick the holly leaves between the foam balls. Add a piece of red or green ribbon around the lid.

This adorable lid cover can be co-ordinated with the flavor of your jams or jellies for a unique gift.

Materials needed:

glue   foam balls
felt   acrylic or poster paint

Cover lid with felt. Make orange, lemon, lime etc. slices by cutting sections from the foam ball. (Can also make cherries, kumquats, etc.) Cover the foam shapes with paper and white glue. When dry paint the colors you want with acrylic or poster paint. Attach to top with glue.

Jams, jellies, other canned foods: Most will keep well for a year or two on your pantry shelf. Check with the giver, though. Some non-processed jams and jellies require refrigeration and they should be popped into your freezer if you can't use them within a month or two. It's always wise to label canned and frozen foods with contents and date at the time they are purchased or received.

BERRY SYRUP

Receivers of this gift from your can cupboard will find it both unusual and delicious. Simple to fix, it keeps indefinitely in sealed jars.

1 quart berry juice (blackberry, raspberry, etc.)	1 tsp. cloves
2 cups sugar	1 tsp. cinnamon
1 tsp. allspice	1 tsp. nutmeg

Mix ingredients in a saucepan and bring to a boil. Boil 15-20 minutes and remove from heat. Put in jars and seal to keep.

MRS. G. K. LEEMON, JR., ASHEVILLE, N. C.

CHOCOLATE SAUCE

Super simple chocolate sauce always good to have on hand for holiday entertaining.

1 square unsweetened chocolate	1 cup sugar
½ stick butter	1 small can evaporated milk (5⅓ oz.)

Melt chocolate and butter over low heat. Add sugar and milk. Bring to a boil stirring constantly. Stores for weeks in refrigerator. Reheat when ready to serve.

MRS. VANCE W. BRABHAM, III

HENRY BAIN STEAK SAUCE

What a delightful gift to give. Keeps indefinitely under refrigeration.

1 bottle Heinz Chili Sauce (12 oz.)	1-17 oz. bottle of Chutney (Major Gray)
1 bottle ketchup (10 oz.)	May have to use 2-8 oz. sizes.
1 bottle A-1 sauce (10 oz.)	¼ cup bourbon
1 bottle worcestershire sauce (10 oz.)	Tobasco to taste

Mix all ingredients and store in refrigerator.

BETTY BETTS

RAISIN SAUCE FOR HAM

1 cup raisins	¼ tsp. salt
1 cup water	pinch of black pepper
5 whole cloves	1 T. butter
¾ cup brown sugar	1 T. vinegar
1 tsp. corn starch	¼ tsp. worcestershire sauce

In saucepan cover raisins with water. Add cloves and simmer (not boil) for 10 minutes. Mix the sugar, corn starch, salt and pepper and add to raisins and cloves. Stir until thickened. Add remaining ingredients. Pour over ham.

MRS. RAY L. COX

HONEY, MAPLE, AND EGG BUTTER WHIP

These easy to fix spreads that are great on rolls, pastries, pancakes, biscuits or breads. For an extra special gift treat add a recipe of whip to a loaf of homemade bread.

Honey Butter Whip:

¼ lb. butter   ½ cup honey
½ cup whipping cream

Allow butter to soften. Combine with other ingredients. Whip till fluffy. (Do not beat until stiff or mixture may curdle)

Maple Butter Whip:

½ cup butter   ¼ cup maple syrup

Let butter soften. Combine with syrup and whip till fluffy.

Egg Butter:

1 quart molasses   nutmeg
6 beaten egg yolks

Melt molasses in iron skillet. Add egg yolks. Stir vigorously until mixture reaches a slow boil. Stir in nutmeg to taste. Serve hot or chilled.

MRS. DENNIS MOSSELLER, VALDOSTA, GA.

WINE AND LIQUEUR JELLY

A unique gift idea with numerous interesting variations.

2½ cups sugar   6 oz. can frozen lemonade
1 cup water   concentrate
½ bottle liquid fruit pectin   paraffin

Variations:

For Créme de Menthe Jelly: add ½ cup of the liqueur (green or white)

For Cointreau Jelly: add ½ cup Cointreau, 4 drops yellow and 2 drops red food coloring

For Angostura Jelly: increase water to 1¼ cups water. Add ¼ cup Angostura bitters.

Combine sugar and water in pan; bring to full rolling boil, stirring constantly. Boil hard 1 minute, then remove from heat. Stir in liquid pectin. Add lemonade concentrate and liqueur and mix well. Skim very quickly and pour into sterilized glasses. Cover at once with ⅛ inch layer of hot paraffin.

When making wine jelly: In double boiler combine 2 cups sherry, rosé or burgundy and 3 cups sugar. Place over rapidly boiling water and stir until sugar is dissolved. Remove from heat and stir in ½ bottle liquid fruit pectin. Pour quickly into sterilized glasses and cover at once with ⅛ inch layer of hot paraffin. Makes 5 8-oz. glasses.

MRS. BRYAN EDWARDS

STRAWBERRY PRESERVES

An easy do ahead food gift that is a favorite with everybody. Recipe yields 4 half pints. Secret of success is to shake pan while cooking and cooling the mixture.

> 2 pints strawberries (washed and capped)
> 2 pints sugar

Place one pint of berries and one pint of sugar in a large saucepan. Cook over medium heat to a boil. Boil 10 minutes. Remove from heat and let cool. Add to same pan another pint of berries and another pint of sugar and cook ten minutes more. Remove from heat. Cool well. Skim foam off of the mixture after it has been removed from heat. Pour into sterilized jars and seal with paraffin.

MRS. J. RICHARD MILLER, IV

HOT PEPPER JELLY

This sweet and hot flavor favorite is great with meats. Also delicious served on cream cheese and crackers as an easy, easy hors d'oeuvre. Hot peppers are rough on sensitive, tender hands. You might want to use gloves when cutting up the peppers.

> ¾ cup bell pepper (cut up and seeded)
> ¼ cup hot pepper (cut up)
>
> 1½ cups cider vinegar
> 6 cups sugar
> 1 bottle Certo

Place peppers, both kinds, in blender with ½ cup of vinegar. Turn to high speed until well blended. Place pepper mixture in 4½ qt. saucepan. Rinse blender with remaining vinegar and add to pepper mixture. Next, add sugar. Bring to rolling boil, and, stirring constantly, cook for three minutes. Remove from heat and skim off foam if necessary. Add Certo. Return to heat and boil one minute after the mixture comes to a boil. Pour into sterilized jars and seal. Red or green food coloring can be added if desired. Yields 5 half pint jars.

MRS. JOHN W. BLACK

CRANBERRY CHUTNEY

A relish you'll relish for holiday giving. Delicious served with ham or turkey or with any casserole calling for chutney.

> 2 cups fresh or frozen cranberries
> 2 large pears
> 2½ cups light brown sugar
> 2 cups golden raisins
> 1½ cups cider vinegar
>
> 2 tsp. salt
> 1 T. mixed pickling spices
> 10-12 whole allspice
> 4-5 whole cloves

Rinse cranberries. Peel, core and chop pears. Combine fruits in large saucepan with sugar, raisins, vinegar and salt. Place other spices in a spice bag. Add to fruit mixture. Bring to boil over high heat. Reduce heat to medium, stirring often. Cook 20 minutes. Let cool, cover, and refrigerate. Yields 2½-3 pints.

MRS. JAY A. MILLIGAN

CRANBERRY-WALNUT RELISH

Especially good at Christmas with turkey and pork.

1 lb. fresh cranberries
2 cups sugar
1 cup English walnuts

1 cup orange marmalade
juice of one lemon or lime

Wash and drain cranberries. Put in shallow baking dish and mix with sugar. Cover tightly and bake (350°) for one hour. Chop 1 cup of walnuts (coarsely) and place in smaller pan. Toast in oven with cranberries until light golden brown, about 12 minutes. Remove cranberries from oven and stir in orange marmalade and lemon juice. Stir in nuts. Mix all well and pour in container. Chill before serving.

MRS. ELLIOTT W. STEVENS

SWEET GARLIC PICKLES

A wonderfully easy pickle recipe that takes 30 minutes of your time and keeps 4 months. Requires no seal at all.

1 gallon sour (Mt. Olive) pickles
5 lbs. sugar
½ pint white vinegar

½ box pickling spices
5 sliced garlic cloves

Slice pickles (about ¼″ thick) and cover with ice water for several hours. Drain. Put in deep enamel covered pot. Add other ingredients on top of pickles and let sit until sugar is dissolved. Stir with a wooden spoon several times a day for about six days. Put in sterilized jars, fill with juices and screw on tops. Serve when very cold and crisp.

MRS. STILES R. FIFIELD

GARLIC CLOVES IN OIL

garlic — 2 or more pkgs.   oil

Peel garlic buds — 2 or more pkgs. — and put in an attractive jar filled with oil. Garlic will keep for months and it's very handy not to have to peel each time you use it.

Can also be made in tarragon vinegar. Use white vinegar and put fresh tarragon in each bottle.

MRS. ADAIR M. GRAHAM

FRENCH DRESSING

1 cup sugar	⅓ cup onion juice
1 cup Wesson or Crisco oil	2 tsp. salt
⅔ cup tarragon vinegar	Dash of paprika
Juice of 2 lemons	

Combine all ingredients and shake well.

MRS. JAMES BARBER

Personal Additions

Index

We are also very proud to offer our most popular <u>Out of Our League</u> Cookbook.

★ **First Place Award** — for general layout, design and printing excellence . . . 600 entries from 100 countries.

Over 400 pages — each section indexed.

Kitchen-tested recipes — two years of testing.

Just for you — tips for the beginner and gourmet plus gifts from the kitchen.

Sales Success — over 45,000 now sold nationwide.

4th Printing — Hard cover spiral binding
— same low price as previous printings —

432 pages — illustrated
ISBN - 09605788-0-3

THE JUNIOR LEAGUE OF GREENSBORO
113 S. Elm Street, Greensboro, North Carolina 27401

Send me _____ copies of FLAVORS AND FAVORS at $2.95 per copy plus $.50 for postage and handling and/or _____ copies of OUT OF OUR LEAGUE at $7.95 per copy plus $1.25 for postage and handling. North Carolina residents please add 4% sales tax.

Name _____
<small>Please Print</small>

Street _____

City _____

State _____ Zip _____

Make checks payable to OUT OF OUR LEAGUE. All proceeds from the sale of books are returned to the community through projects of The Junior League of Greensboro.

THE JUNIOR LEAGUE OF GREENSBORO
113 S. Elm Street, Greensboro, North Carolina 27401

Send me _____ copies of FLAVORS AND FAVORS at $2.95 per copy plus $.50 for postage and handling and/or _____ copies of OUT OF OUR LEAGUE at $7.95 per copy plus $1.25 for postage and handling. North Carolina residents please add 4% sales tax.

Name _____
<small>Please Print</small>

Street _____

City _____

State _____ Zip _____

Make checks payable to OUT OF OUR LEAGUE. All proceeds from the sale of books are returned to the community through projects of The Junior League of Greensboro.